AGAINST EVERY HOPE

Against Every Hope

To Susan & Jacobs,
We hope you enjoy reading
our story.

a memoir

INDIA, MOTHER TERESA, AND A BABY GIRL

Bonnie

BONNIE TINSLEY

WordCrafts

CONTENTS

Dedication vii
Acknowledgements ix
Prologue xi

PART I: Against Every Hope 1
  1. How We Got Here 3
      Interlude ~ Postcard from the Electric Cornfield 14
  2. At Home in Southeast Asia 15
      Interlude ~ Gelang-gelang 24
  3. Bound for India 25

PART II: The Climb Begins 31
  4. Darjeeling 33
  5. How High the Mountain? 42
  6. The Mystery Baby 50
      Interlude ~ In the Himalayan Zoo, Darjeeling 57
  7. At Home in Bangalore 59
      Interlude: My Fortune 64
  8. The Politics of Violence 65
      Interlude ~ The Genie of Grant Road Cross 72
  9. Where to Get Help 85
  10. India Fever 96
  11. Mountains of Paperwork 106
  12. Home Leave 116
  13. To Calcutta with Love 132
  14. The Last Hope 138
  15. The Good News 145
  16. Reversal 151
      Interlude ~ Reversal 156
  17. Long Distance Calling God 157
      Interlude ~ The Beggars' Carnival 166

PART III: Too Much to Hope 169

    18. Almost Ours 171

        Interlude ~ Pema's Song in the key of D 180

    19. Announcement 181

    20. Citizenship 192

        Interlude ~ Jungle Glider 203

    21. Back Home in Singapore and Thereafter 204

        Interlude ~ Covenant 217

    22. Epilogue 218

DEDICATION

To Dorothy Christena Gibbs,
best girlfriend, mentor, and godmother to Pema,
beloved teacher to thousands in Dubuque schools
during her 30-year tenure,
the one who guided me and untold others
through life's exigencies with consummate
goodness, intelligence, and grace

in memoriam

Passage to more than India!
Are thy wings plumed indeed for such far flights?

Walt Whitman, "Passage to India"

~

Life never gives us what we want at the moment that we consider
appropriate. Adventures do occur, but not punctually.

E. M. Forster, *A Passage to India*

ACKNOWLEDGEMENTS

The first person to thank would have to be my loving and patient husband, Cliff Richeson, for all that he does for me especially in the way of memory bank and technical guru. Next in line to her Dad would be our daughter Pema, who remains the light and inspiration of my life.

Thank you to fellow writers Connie Foster, Debbie McClanahan, Diana Revell, Peggy Duke, and to teaching colleagues Martha Millsaps and Sissy Woodall, who kindly read and re-read the manuscript in various drafts over the past seven years. Thank you to Kathy Anderson for helping me navigate social media. Thank you to Gretchen Liu in Singapore whose insightful editing suggestions turned me in the right direction. And a special word of thanks to Jenny Gibbs Castro who channeled her Mother's gifts (see Dedication page) and her own amazing creative energy into what is now the finished product. Above all others, Jenny's belief in the power of our story and her fresh take on it in the last draft gave me the hope I needed to finish the book. And finally, thank you to Mike Parker and his team at WordCrafts Press for recognizing the value in my book and delivering it to readers.

The excerpt from *Mother Teresa: Come Be My Light; The Private Writings of the Saint of Calcutta* © by the Mother Teresa Center, exclusive licensee throughout the world of the Missionaries of Charity for the works of Mother Teresa. Used with permission.

We owe Sister M. Dionysia an eternal debt of gratitude for the trust and guidance she gave us on this blessed journey. After 20 years being out of touch, Cliff was able to find Sr. Dionysia with the help of Google maps and Skype and to speak to her in India at her current assignment at the Missionaries of Charity Nirmal Hriday Bhavan Home for the Destitute and Dying in Srikakulam, Andhra Pradesh. He let her know how very grateful we are for the loving Pema received while in Sr. Dionysia's care.

PROLOGUE

She phones home at least once a week, on average.

"How's it going, Mom?" starts these conversations. She is a little breathless. I can hear her heels tapping the pavement even over the phone static, on the way from the shuttle to her office at Stanford University. I fill in the pauses with news of my week here in Tennessee. I mention sighting the blue heron on the Greenway again and that feeling of being touched by the magic she and I have shared. I wait for her spill.

The new job has its challenges. At this writing, Pema is newly arrived at Stanford's Department of Pathology. When she was Director of Operations for the Alzheimer's Disease Research Center and Udall Center at the University of Washington, she was in charge of millions in grant money. That job suited her. She excels at telling people what to do in a nice way. But the new job at Stanford offers the potential for an international stage, which she prefers.

She has been packing her bag for world travel since age five. Her Dad and I could not be more proud of her burgeoning career. And she is so beautiful, even strangers approach her with marriage proposals. There was a time, however, when this dazzling young

woman was not our daughter, nor had we any hope whatsoever
of having her—even in our dreams.

~

She was tucked away inside a crib, a sickly-looking baby almost buried under an odd assortment of handmade quilts and blankets. As I remember it, the large room was almost empty, except for that crib in a dark corner. So hushed and separated from the other orphanage activity, this may have served as the sick room. If anyone had spoken, the room would have echoed. When the nuns finally unearthed the baby from that mismatched pile of wool and brought her into the daylight, she was crying. Her eyes were pinched shut against the sunlight, probably because she rarely saw the sun from her night-shrouded corner of the world. Something black like charcoal cast dark lines across her forehead, and the full crop of dark brown hair on top of her head was slicked down with oil.

When the girl in plaited pigtails finally released her into my arms, my heart lifted up like the heron unfolds her broad sweep of wings and takes flight. The baby felt solid and feverish. She smelled yeasty, like a loaf of bread fresh from the oven. She was wearing many layers, right down to her fingertips. They were long fingers, like those of a baby destined to play the piano or wield a paintbrush. She was 10-days-old and had come to Mother Teresa's orphanage from Victoria Hospital, where she had been abandoned after birth. Victoria was Darjeeling's one and only full-service hospital probably since the Victorian era. What looked to me like bruising darkened her wrists and ankles.

I have replayed this scene over and over, watching the long legs of a blue heron wading on the water's edge, head and beak thrust forward and then back as she marks each tentative step. The moment and the heron are playing in slow motion, in black and white. I move along the threshold, look inside that off-limits room and know somehow this moment will change my life forever, whether I want it to or not. I ask to see the baby inside that crib. The nuns move towards it. The girl in pigtails picks her up. We all move into the daylight, into Technicolor. In the photograph, I am wearing a bright green wool sweater with red plaid grosgrain ribbon running down the front. I am looking down at the fussy baby in my arms and smiling. At this moment, I want my barren life to change.

~

Even though the peaks of Mount Kanchenjunga were snow-covered in November, it was not yet the winter season in Darjeeling. The nuns assured me that before winter set in, the babies would be taken down the mountain to Tindharia, where the weather was more hospitable. There was a tea plantation there converted into another Missionaries of Charity orphanage, also under the care of Mother Teresa.

"Oh, the father is here. You came to see your daughter," they shouted when my husband Cliff finally arrived to check out the baby. It wasn't that he was adverse to the baby, only that it was a hard climb to reach the orphanage. Actually as soon as he took one look at her, he was totally smitten. They gave us instructions on how to reach the M.C. convent and office complex called the Motherhouse in Calcutta to begin the adoption process. So we dropped everything, and off we went buoyed up by their enthusiasm. We had already arranged for delivery of a crib and a stash of baby clothes with friends in Bangalore, where we were living at the time. And we had already named her Pema, the Tibetan word for "lotus flower." There was a huge enclave of Tibetan refugees in Darjeeling, and all Pema's features looked Tibetan to us—her lovely dark brown hair and dark, almond-shaped eyes—when she would let us see them.

~

At Calcutta's Motherhouse, a fleet of young women in saris were down on hands and knees scrubbing the floors, the strong smell of Clorox biting the air. The head of adoptions for the Missionaries of Charity, Sister Margaret Mary, made her way towards us stepping around them. She was short in stature but monumental in the power of her authority behind the clipboard. Nonetheless we had every expectation of acing this one, given our credentials. Mother Teresa would not have to look elsewhere for a family for Pema. Here we were, holding numerous degrees between us, perfectly suitable parents residing right here in India with the wealth and weight of Cliff's U.S. based company supporting us over the next two years, not to mention his guaranteed career path in Southeast Asia.

After a brief interrogation session giving us no question as to who was in charge, Margaret Mary was quick to point out all the strikes against us. Mother Teresa's organization was no longer giving babies to Americans, only to Catholic countries—Belgium, Italy, and France. We were Americans. We weren't Catholic. Cliff, a one-time altar boy, was now following the path of Buddhism, and I was an attending Quaker.

"What's that?" Sr. Margaret Mary wanted to know and then didn't give me the space to answer. She obviously did not like me. Also I was divorced from my first husband. Strike number three. She let us know that her Sneha /our Pema was destined for Belgium, when she reached the age of two. And no, we could not see Mother Teresa. She was not available.

The tiny nun determined to stand in the way of our happiness did not get it. We loved that baby and wanted to care for her now, now when she most needed the love and affection of parents in the present. Why take a chance on her surviving myriad diseases and unknown living conditions in a series of orphanages until she reached the age of two, when who knows what unknowns might await her in Belgium? And how did she get those bruises on her wrists and ankles? Who was protecting this baby now?

A picture of the boy David confronting the giant Goliath from the Bible-story pages of my childhood flashed through my head. There was nothing we could do but turn away and leave the Motherhouse and the unsmiling Indian woman who just destroyed all our hope for a family. It felt like just the two of us, Cliff and I, withstanding the mighty forces of the Catholic Church with no stone in sight.

PART I
AGAINST EVERY HOPE

Chapter 1

HOW WE GOT HERE
A LOVE STORY

The notion of a baby Pema, plus this most unlikely road to motherhood, is the farthest thing from our imaginations when we are posted to India in 1983. How did we reach this troubled land in the first place? In truth, I believe the fault is mine. When Cliff's boss offers us India following our two-year stint in Singapore, I am the one who urges Cliff to accept it, even though he is reluctant. It is rumored that no one in the company is willing to go to India, much less take their families. Both living and working conditions are said to be too harsh. But just the year before, the film "Gandhi" had been released in Singapore and I can think of nowhere else I want to be than India. By comparison, Singapore feels like the tiny island it is, and India—vast, energetic, and the most important place on earth at this time. David Lean is reported to be filming E. M. Forster's "A Passage to India" in Bangalore, our next overseas destination, should Cliff accept it.

~

To give a full-on picture of how we got to India, I would have to go back seven years to the very beginning, to the night Cliff and I met. Like most of the stories I tell about my husband, this one makes me laugh.

I was standing in line ready to pay the fees and finish registration for graduate school. When I realized that I had missed a step in the long, drawn-out process, I turned around to the man standing behind me. He was close to my height, with longish dark hair and neatly trimmed moustache. I noticed he was peering at my open checkbook through wide-rimmed, very thick glasses. He looked harmless enough. I was to find out later that he was hoping I was single, and the number of names on the checkbook would tell him that.

"Would you mind saving my place in line? Looks like I skipped a step."

"I'll guard it with my life," he said, with a very straight face. Now, there is a different come-on, I thought, and could not help smiling to myself. I went to finish the step I missed and returned to find the line even longer with my guardian still at his post.

"Would you like to get a cup of coffee when we finish here?" he said.

"Looks like I owe you one for saving my place in line." But every coffee spot we checked at the student union was closed by this time.

"I know where we can get a beer, just across the street," he said.

"There are no bars across the street."

"It's as good as a bar, and the beer is free. It's where I live." Cliff was sharing the old frame house across from the University Union with three other veterans. Over beer and conversation with his roommates, we immediately recognized the wanderlust in each other. I was freshly divorced and headed to Mexico City to study Cervantes at UNAM with the hope of becoming a translator. He had left a career with the Jeep Corporation to prepare for his dream of returning to Hong Kong, where he had spent his R&R on leave from Vietnam, but this time to live and work overseas.

Like too many of his generation who had risked their lives in Vietnam, Cliff came home to no welcoming parades. Due to the unpopularity of "the war" and by association its veterans, he was warned not to speak of his war experience to neighbors or possible employers. All the ribbons, medals, decorations, and badges he had earned in combat and was so proud of were now objects of derision. His mother sold them in a yard sale.

After serving as a rifleman in a recon-ready-reaction platoon with the legendary First Infantry Division, he found life in America foreign and without purpose. With his platoon in Vietnam, he was part of a brotherhood known only to men who face death together and trust each other with their lives. In the short four-day passage from his last jungle patrol to arrival at his parents' home, he had suffered loss of purpose, identify, and family. Between his base camp at Phu Loi, Vietnam and his old home in Peoria, his status had changed from a soldier making life-or-death decisions on a daily basis, capable of keying his radio handset and calling in air strikes and gunships, to a factory floor-sweep in the local Caterpillar plant. That was his only job offer. He took advantage of the GI bill to finish his engineering degrees so that he could go back to the part of the world where he felt most at home, Southeast Asia, and where he could make a contribution that mattered. He had to bide his time before Vietnam and his friends there would be open to his visits. In the meantime, I was beyond grateful that Cliff had survived the war intact and with a spirit of adventure that would turn my life around. Only much later would we have to acknowledge my wounded warrior's PTSD.

I liked him for even more reasons than I can remember now. I can still see the photo hanging in his office. It was taken on R&R in Hong Kong in 1968. My heart went out to the small Chinese girl pulling on the sculling oar of a sampan while her two brothers are begging for coins from the tourists in Hong Kong harbor.

I found his mid-western-grown honesty refreshing. I liked his corny, often repeated jokes, usually inspired by the classics, like this Euripides joke.

"You rippa deez jeans and you won't get another pair." Or the joke on *cogito ergo sum*.

"Descartes goes into a bar. He takes a stool and the bartender asks him if he wants a beer. Descartes hesitates then replies 'I think not' and immediately disappears." Or the many jokes about his imaginary Uncle Morrie. My favorite: "My Uncle Morrie went blind in one eye from drinking coffee. He kept forgetting to take the spoon out of the cup." He could play with words, make outrageous connections, and lighten any moment with his off-the-wall humor, sometimes inspired by Jonathan Winters. Even though I had a distinct distaste for the off-colored jokes, it might have been the way he told them that made even those jokes endearing. Maybe Cliff seemed like the funniest man alive because there hadn't been much laughter in my first marriage those last years.

Another thing in his favor, I liked his size because it was like mine, only more solid and muscular. A friend commented that we looked like "a pair of book ends." I liked his patience in getting me to bed. In fact, I had to make the first move. Once I did, kiss him that is, we were most decidedly a couple. I wonder if he knew that his gentle, patient approach had the effect of gaining my confidence and trust, which was never more evident than in our most intimate times together. We called it "Muskrat Love" after the Captain and Tennille song popular at the time. And I liked the special interest he took in my little super-mini R5, the orange Renault he called my "roller skate." I deemed it my trophy for having survived the ten-year marriage and divorce.

I thought I was doing the right thing in marrying my college sweetheart. All the key players in my life were expecting the marriage, especially my mother who had been keeping track of all my school friends' marriages. My previous experience dating was limited. I was a virgin in the first degree and full of reservations going down the aisle. It was a marriage five years in the making, firmly footed in shared friends and idyllic campus experiences surrounded by ivy-covered walls. When we separated after an accumulated 15 years, I felt betrayed, yes, but also un-caged, or more like shot out of a cannon into the waiting arms of the seventh fleet on shore leave. Men came out of the woodwork, even my husband's colleagues, professing long-time closeted attraction. So much attention helped to bolster my self-confidence, for a while. If it had not been for the powerful influence of my overly protective mother, appearing like a specter in my dreams, and the cautionary tales I was raised on, I am sure I would have totally lost all my accumulated wifely virtue.

For a long time, I did not take Cliff very seriously, perhaps because he was trying so hard to make me laugh. There had been several other suitors. But from the start I trusted him;

with him I was in my safe place. Eventually he won me over by sheer persistence and the promise of adventure. He was going places, and I wanted to go places, too. He could fix things, anything, from my little car to the leaky faucet and air conditioner in my apartment. And most impressive of all, he could build a fire, I mean from scratch, with one match, not from some quick starter.

My happiest memories of those early dating days were the camping trips to Indiana's Brown County. He would park his red Jeep Cherokee near a stream, pitch his two-man tent and then search for kindling wood. He was meticulous in choosing the size of kindling: small twigs for the starter pile in the shape of a teepee, and then sticks and branches and logs selected in graduating sizes. The building of each fire looked to me like a work of art. Only later did I recognize the OCD tendency.

Over the next few years, we explored most of the nearby state parks and national forests and then affordable Mexico, from mountainous San Miguel de Allende to the beaches of the Mexican Caribbean. We checked out the color festival spectacles in Mexico City and spent the long end of a summer camping at archaeological sites from Oaxaca's Monte Alban to Palenque (the roar of jaguars keeping us awake at night) to Chichen Itza and Uxmal ruins in the Yucatan and as far as the end of the Yucatan Peninsula. By then it was easy. Just open the red Jeep's tail gate, bring out Cliff's hand-made kitchen box, set up the mountain cook stove, and we had the makings of *huevos rancheros*. No telling how many eggs we ate all across Mexico.

Then after too many nights in the tent, Cliff says he remembers a scene something like this that took place at

Villahermosa. As he tells it, I am chopping tomatoes and onions with his hunting knife for yet another meal of *huevos rancheros*. The sky is darkening, presaging rain. More menacing than the sky, a dark mass of birds fills the palm trees just above our heads with Hitchcock dramatic intensity. I am tired and begin gesturing and punctuating my conversation with the knife. Cliff interprets my knife-wielding as a threat on his life and a pressing need to find a hotel. We load up the Jeep as the rains begin to fall and head for the first hotel we can find.

It is gorgeous. We step out of the dark and rain into a spectacle of light. The lobby is adorned with distinctive Mexican hand-blown glass panels falling in cascading tiers of chandelier above us from three stories up. It was not just any hotel, but a top-of-the-line, five-star with a bar-cum-pool and beds supported on bamboo culms the size of elephant trunks. I sleep, really sleep, for the first time in days. I am a happy camper.

Across hundreds of unmapped miles of Mexico together, just the two of us, I can count only four "incidents" or near-crises that might have jeopardized our relationship. To begin, in Mexico City a traffic cop looking for a free lunch pulled us over at one of those ubiquitous round-a-bouts. Holding a leatherette pouch full of US dollars, he kept pointing to the plastic sign listing possible traffic offenses in English. He accused us of driving on the left, when we should have been on the right, or *viceversa*. In my best classroom Spanish, I managed to talk the *policia* out of the charge by repeatedly insisting on taking the matter up with his superior. Truth to tell, Cliff just slipped the guy a pack of Pall Malls, and we were on our way.

Number two, our suitcases were stolen out of the locked Jeep in Puebla; we were just too trusting. Fortunately, they had the courtesy to leave us our camping gear. And number three, I lost my right contact lens celebrating my first view of the Pacific. Actually, to be exact, we were on a pier at Salina Cruz that jutted into the Gulf of Tehuantepec that runs into the Ocean. Cliff made the mistake of reaching for me to celebrate the moment and knocked the hard contact lens out of my eye between the planks of the pier into the murky deep below. After that, the tension could be felt right down to the tread on our tires.

Number four, little did we know that Cliff's red Jeep Cherokee with the winch on the front bumper was a moving target all across Mexico. One time we were pulled over on the road to Merida at an internal checkpoint not far from the border with Guatemala. The border patrolman paced around the Jeep several times looking in the windows as if for contraband. He told Cliff to open all the doors. He climbed in and made a cursory search of the interior. Finally he climbed out, stood spread-legged in front of the bumper bearing the winch, and squinted at Cliff with hands on hips.

"I am trying to figure out a way to impound your car, but I can't. I'd love to have your car," he said and smiled in that conspiratorial way that only a Mexican *federale* can smile. Then he shrugged his shoulders and *adios*, we were on our way again. But this was Mexico in the safe '70s, not India in the '80s.

We made it as far as Isla Mujeres at the tip of the Yucatan peninsula when a telegram from his mother called Cliff home. His Dad had been hospitalized with a heart attack. The return to Illinois was uneventful, except for three days in Vera Cruz where I thought I would lose Cliff to a deadly case of Montezuma's revenge. In spite of that, even today we agree that we loved Mexico so much—the landscape, the welcoming people, the food, the endless adventuring—we might still be there if it had not been for that telegram and worry over Cliff's dad.

~

In October 1980, Cliff and I were married in the backyard of our little brick bungalow in Indianapolis. Joining us were only a few family members from Cliff's side, our neighbors, and our resident chipmunks. I guess marriage had always been a possibility for us and should not have but did take on more urgency after my father's dour pronouncement.

"You know, you're not getting any younger, honey." This elicited all sorts of soul-searching on my part. The quality of marriage in my family had been strained at best. My mother was a very late 30 when I was born. She divorced my father a few years later when she could no longer tolerate his philandering. I can still remember their parting of ways in the tiny kitchen of our row-house. I was standing at the end of the cot set up temporarily in the dining room. Daddy kept reaching to hold my mother, doing his best to try to make amends, and Mother kept turning her back on him, dismissing his sort of loose overtures. Only later could I see what the toddler missed. My father was in one of his normal states of inebriation.

I always found it interesting that Daddy insisted I stay and look after my totally capable and self-sufficient mother even after college graduation. He had no real compunctions about moving out all those years ago. And then, of course, I had followed the family pattern with a divorce at age 33, except for me it was a relief to have no children. In fact, if I had wanted children, the desire came as vague imaginings born out of loneliness in an old farmhouse on the edge of an Illinois cornfield in the very isolation I had chosen. My husband who was a sculptor was teaching at the university in town. I was trying to be a writer, plus subsistence farmer. Interesting how the "Back-to-Earth" movement conveniently coincided with the Women's Movement. Little did I know what was changing women's lives while I was picking hornworms off tomato vines. *Our Bodies, Ourselves* was a real revelation.

Set on 10 acres of land on Sugar Creek with a barn to accommodate building sculpture, the prairie frame was built at turn-of-century with a wide front porch meant for rockers—my first-ever home since the one I grew up in Virginia. It didn't matter that the house was rumored to be haunted. The last woman who lived in it had died in the bathtub from mysterious causes. To me, it was the writer's haven I had been dreaming of surrounded by the wildlife that invested my poetry—like the meadow larks exchanging whistles across the fields, those ethereal notes resounding from their bright yellow breasts as if in an echo chamber. There were families of skunk, too. The mother would parade her brood of five or six black-on-white miniatures most prominently against the winter snow. There were peach trees, grape arbors, garden patches already laid out (presumably by the woman who died in the bathtub), and most memorable of all, the pear tree dressed in white bridal splendor every springtime. It was harder to leave that old house than to leave the marriage. After the house had been sold, I still remember the day I went back to dig a hole deep enough to bury my wedding rings beside the pear tree.

Cliff, on the other hand, had been a carefree, dedicated

bachelor his whole life. He knew for certain that he had fathered no children. He was happy to have his brother Bob do that. Bob and wife Denise had produced two girls and then quit when they had the requisite boy. I fell in love with their children but was less than eager to have my own just yet, in spite of my father's warning. Cliff and I needed more time together.

For the simple wedding ceremony, Cliff was all suited up in gray with a vest even, and I was wearing a long-sleeved teal-green silk dress that just covered my knees. He was his usual "not taking any of this too seriously" self. In the photograph of our official toast with champagne glasses full, however, the flash captures his unmistakable "deer-in-the-headlights" look. That was just before my piece of pizza landed tomato-sauce-side-down in my lap. Brother Bob rushed the dress to the cleaners, but it never looked quite the same. We sent out our wedding announcement on picture postcards of Indianapolis, popularly labeled then the "electric cornfield," because of the Indy 500 Raceway that lit up the night for miles around, I am guessing.

POSTCARD FROM THE ELECTRIC CORNFIELD

Here, we live in a red brick
house in the woods
between a lake and a gravel pit.
We remark to the other
each time the geese fly over.
As elsewhere
the rain slants down
taking dead limbs with it
to the ground.
We take our vitamin C.
Sometimes
after many days together
we do not speak
through dinner.
Here, they drive faster:
the distances are greater.
As elsewhere, the people
are alternately
gracious and suspicious.
Yesterday the pump broke.
Now we bathe
in brown water
and touch each other
in new places.
We get regular mail delivery.
Come
visit.

Chapter 2
AT HOME IN SOUTHEAST ASIA

I like to believe that about the time we are headed for Southeast Asia circumstances are conspiring to produce the baby Pema. A young private-school girl is falling in love with a young man in the very Darjeeling where Mother Teresa fulfilled her novitiate. It's entirely possible that the girl is a student at the Loreto Convent School where Mother spent her first two years in India. The children of British families as well as a few from wealthy Indian families attend the School.

The story of these young lovers would be written along the lines of Romeo and Juliet or Pyramis and Thisbe set in the Himalayas. The well-to-do parents of the girl reject the young man's lesser tribal family, perhaps Tibetan, which makes their love burn even more brightly. At some point in her orphanage history, Pema is marked with a red tikka on her forehead between her eyes. The Sisters must think she is Hindu and therefore Indian, or they may be hoping for a local adoption, even though her features appear more and more Nepali/Tibetan as she grows. The fact remains that her family has the wear-with-all to use Darjeeling's Victoria Hospital for the birth and then remove the mother from the baby girl. These are only imaginings, of course. The Sisters

*have no information available on the baby, except that she was
born around first November 1984 at Victoria Hospital and then
abandoned.*

~

In the spring of 1981, Cliff got the call from his new
employer, a competitor of Caterpillar called WABCO, West-
inghouse Airbrake, the Haulpak Division, to "troubleshoot"
for the company in Southeast Asia. His official title was
Regional Service Representative for Southeast Asia. The hub
of all that activity, Singapore, would be our home for the next
two years, if we agreed to the move.

In those days, companies were anxious to have the families of their employees fully supportive of their overseas
assignments. So I was flown to Singapore first-class Pan Am
sharing that rarefied space, the linen table cloth, white-gloved
service, champagne, and caviar with only one other first-class
passenger. Graying at the temples, his long legs comfortably
stretched out in gray flannel trousers and loafers, Jim Miller
looked every bit the part of CEO of a company supporting
the oil industry, a seasoned veteran of Southeast Asia. I was
also in appropriate costume, I thought, dressed in the only
white linen suit I could find in the style of Ingrid Bergman
when Bogart sees her off on the air-strip in *Casablanca*.

Under the influence of too much champagne, I shared my
worries about my future. He assured me that there was no
way I might be mistaken for an "ugly American" because we
expats were responsible for the growth and prosperity of Asia,
by golly. We were there with a mission, to do our part to make
the whole world a better place. I can't recall precisely, but I
think he might have introduced a few well-chosen Biblical
verses to bolster his argument.

Cliff was already on the job in Western Australia. Even though we had not talked with each other for over three weeks even by phone, I expected him to meet me on my arrival at the airport. For too long I could not locate him. I can still recall my level of anxiety, followed by that crucial meeting as if it were an old movie still playing in my mind. It was the old Paya Lebar Airport, rumored to be ghost-infested and soon to be replaced by Changi International, Singapore's space-age, chrome-encrusted pagoda in the sky. Planters full of orchids would soon replace the concrete bench Cliff had been sleeping on while he was awaiting my arrival in the polite company of rats the size of cats. I wondered how I must have looked after 24 hours without sleep between D.C. and San Francisco, then Honolulu, then Hong Kong and now Singapore. Exactly what country was I in? "The country of airport" was the only name I could give it.

My luggage was marked with priority handling. It was among the first to come off the conveyor belt. I had felt a singular kind of priority throughout the trip, not just in the first-class compartment but in the loneliness and uncertainty that comes with being taken care of, with having no power to assert my presence, except to order more champagne. I was protected in the first degree, like my luggage, but also powerless in determining my future should I arrive in this totally strange place with no one there to meet me. I may as well have been a stow-away hidden in a wooden box in the cargo hold, the question less where I was going than when will someone, friend or foe, let me out. And did I have a right to be in Singapore like the early immigrants who had work waiting for them? We had been forewarned that I would not be able to work; I would be riding on Cliff's coattails with a dependent visa. Soon the glare and tropical humidity were pressing down on me as if I were carrying my suitcase on top of my head.

At last I could pick Cliff out from all the dark-headed masses straining at heels and necks. He was slightly taller and his bulk stood out naturally among the smaller, thinner Asians. The glass doors between us slid open easily. The men at the desk he had been talking with made a gesture to restrain any passage either way through the open doors. Cliff shrugged, and I returned to the circulating belts of luggage. I located a cart somehow and wheeled my luggage from the table check to the doorway and put my arms around the familiar sweat-soaked body. I pressed against him and found his mouth. I stayed with that mouth with a purpose, even when he kept trying to make short staccato kisses, husband kisses for the airport personnel. I kept insisting. I wanted a lasting contact that would not break off into more required formality. I wanted his body and his mouth to form a kind of lingering seal, the pressure that lovers stamp on each other, not for permanence but for passion, for nothing but desire and the moment's urgent need. Later I came to understand that such public displays of affection were frowned upon in Asia.

"Hey, there will be plenty of time for that," he said, taking the cart and signaling toward the taxi stand.

~

For a week the company housed us in the suite of a five-star hotel on Singapore's main shopping thoroughfare Orchard Road while we searched for an apartment and to see how I liked it. Tropical palm-studded, pool-sided, clean and green Singapore, Asia's expat paradise—what was there not to like?

Well, cockroaches, for one, large air-borne cockroaches that might easily pass for birds. Since Cliff wasn't a part of the sales staff, we did not warrant penthouse accommodations, which were located above their flight-path. Instead we settled for a three bedroom flat with attached baths spread over three levels, and a wide balcony across the living room draped with purple bougainvillea overlooking the swimming pool and tennis courts. Like I said, what was there not to like? For the first time, I would have the freedom to indulge my passion for plants and museums and the time to write uninterrupted. No worries about work; the company was paying most of the bills. Cliff and I could look seriously into starting a family. At the end of the week, we returned to Indianapolis to store and pack for the move and then flew back to Singapore to await our shipment. But Cliff was already on the job. We arrived jet-lagged at the hotel at 2:00 a.m. He had a flight to Jakarta, Indonesia at noon. I found his note on the dresser when I saw daylight. It was scrawled in large letters with a marker on lined paper:

"Bonnie, you are beautiful!! I love you! Cliff"

~

After a couple weeks alone in the hotel with Cliff on the road and no access to communication, I decided to move into our partially furnished flat. Almost as soon as I had walked in and closed the front door, I heard the doorbell ring. A flower vendor was kneeling before a plastic sheet unfolding at my feet a rainbow-colored assortment of long-stemmed orchids like nothing I had ever seen before, hundreds of them. I filled the empty spaces of our apartment with vases of orchids for a few dollars. Their freshness lasted for weeks. What was there not to like about Singapore?

Like I said, cockroaches. That night I pulled back the curtains and threw open the wide bedroom window to the tropical night air, turned off the light, and crawled into bed beside my first resident cockroach. To say I was hysterical was putting it mildly.

"Are you alright down there?" worried voices in different accents from nearby balconies shouted out in the darkness.

"Yes, I'm okay, just an overly-friendly cockroach." I remember living in the company of cockroaches in a house in eastern Kentucky, but they weren't of this magnitude, nor were they so much a presence. The cockroaches I was familiar with were the creepy-crawly kind, low-liers that usually kept to themselves in damp basements and cupboards unless disturbed by the daylight. So far as I can remember, they did not fly.

I phoned the one number I had been given, the company's bachelor salesman and self-styled life-of-the-party Bill Wagner. I demanded to know where Cliff was and when he would be back in Singapore. Bill didn't have a whole lot of sympathy.

"Hey, girl, just get used to it. This is Singapore. This is the tropics. Besides, what's the difference, Cliff or a cockroach in your bed?"

What I learned early on in our overseas experience was not to depend on Cliff's presence, even if he had a fixed schedule to be in Singapore and I was privy to it. When Cliff finally returned, he explained that what was supposed to be a week-long trip to get the equipment up and running took more than three weeks because, among other delays, it took three days just to reach the work site. Cliff's working life/our joint life was at the mercy of mostly unpredictable third-world travel, terrain, and culture.

To reach the little mining town of Soroako in south Sulawesi, Indonesia, you fly first to Jakarta and then catch the next day's flight to Ujung Pandang and then overnight there or stay until you can get manifested on the De Havilland Otter, the Canadian bush plane that takes you over the Bay of Bone to land at an airstrip in the heart of the jungle. Sulawesi, formerly known as the Celebes, is that island east of Borneo in the Indonesian archipelago shaped like a cat about to dive into the Makassar Strait and waving a long ribbon-like tail. It rains two inches every day of the year in Soroako, and the Celebes apes cross the road in troops like they own the place.

The equipment waiting for Cliff's attendance lay 35 miles down the mountain at the port of Malili, more jungle creek than port. Meanwhile work had been delayed because of the Ramadan holiday, even though the crew kept at it in spite of the fast. Cliff's visa needed renewing, and that took another couple of days. Bill had sold the mining equipment to a Canadian buyer, but he had no knowledge whatsoever of their location or how to get there or what he had sold them. He told Cliff the machines were ready to roll, but in fact they were shipped as a complete knock-down, or in pieces that had to be assembled. Thus the sometimes tense relationship between company sales and service staff members.

My reward after all that distress and worry was the safe return of my husband bearing gifts--a set of beautiful bamboo hand-woven mats and tapestry and a magical bracelet from a Gelang-gelang tree rooted in the Bay of Bone. The complexity and long endurance of that assignment was only the beginning. I soon learned that at this stage Cliff's territory included not only all of the Indonesian Archipelago, but also Australia, Burma, Cambodia, Korea, Malaysia, the Philippines, Sri Lanka, Thailand, Vietnam, and wherever else the Company saw fit to send him. Home for the weekend wasn't even an option, nor was there any promise of my accompanying him. I had to give up my own travel narrative for the questionable comforts of expat living—the shopping, the tanning, the lunching, the ladies clubbing. Something told me I needed to look for work.

One of my Quaker friends from the U. K. who had been free-lancing for Singapore's English-language newspaper *The Straits Times* introduced me to the editor of the feature pages. Jane Perkins was a tall, stunning dark-haired Brit "gone native" in Chinese *shang sam* and chopsticks neatly tieing up her chignon. She had come to Singapore with a portfolio from major magazines in London, Sydney, and Hong Kong. Jane seemed rather skeptical of yet another aspiring expat wife/writer until I submitted my first piece to the paper on yes, cockroaches, "The Care and Feeding of Your Cockroach" complete with a cartoon sketch. And when she learned I could write about art, I became a regular on the review pages. Eventually she invited us into her select circle of friends.

I could not believe my luck. My historical articles on the Singapore Botanic Gardens, coupled with my volunteer work there, culminated in a book contract with Times Books International. *Singapore Green: A History and Guide to the Singapore Botanic Gardens* was published shortly before we had to leave for India. My poetry had been published in literary journals in the Midwest, but this was my very first book. Only after returning from India many months later did I see it on display at the Changi Airport newsstand and then in bookstores all over Singapore. Proud first-time author that I was, I made a point of visiting every bookstore in the city just to see the bright and shiny green soft-bound, sized just right for holding in the hand and walking about the Gardens. I had taken the opportunity to dedicate the book to my mother. After all, it was her admiration and respect for "God's green earth" that had inspired mine. And Cliff as photographer joined in the celebration. His image on the cover—a lotus flower fully unfurled like a pedestal holding the iconic Gardens band-stand, a nice piece of trick photography—probably helped sell the book.

Interlude

GELANG-GELANG

Under the Bay of Bone
down under
the nudging fish
and current swirls
on the bottom shelf
they grow coiled
like snakes,
knotty as slim twigs
from sea-breathing trees
rooted
to the belly
of the bay of bone.
And the Bugis divers
dreaming treasure
and the lovers
know their magic
with nets and sails
who trade so deep
the demon mines
and weedy tomb
of the Bay of Bone
far as breath will go
they go down
and down
with nothing
but a sea-bone
round the wrist
and never drown.

Chapter 3

BOUND FOR INDIA

F*or six years, Cliff and I live together with no sign of any-thing like pregnancy. And with the full knowledge that I was not impregnated at any time throughout a prior ten-year marriage mostly absent the pill, we decide to seek the aid of one of Singapore's most prominent fertility specialists. Nothing like adoption enters our minds, and certainly no anticipation of the miracle of a Baby Pema. When we are bound for India, I am looking at age forty and still hopeful, even given the bad news from the fertility tests, Cliff's erratic travel schedule, and so much time apart.*

~

In Cliff's absence during those two years in Singapore, I spread my time between research on the Botanic Gardens, free-lance work on the newspaper, and volunteering as a docent with the Friends of the Museum. The two-story National Museum was a treasure trove of regional antiquities that represented the history and culture of Singapore. I had grown up with the Smithsonian which was a good deal grander, but that museum had none of this stuff, best I could remember. Although China may have contributed the greatest flow of immigrants to the tiny Island, India was the dominant influence in Southeast Asia because of the waves of Indian traders and immigrants beginning as early as the third and continuing up until the fifteenth century CE Singapore formed the geographic and cultural hub of all that, and they were proud to display that priority status in their National Museum.

Among the many wax-printed *batiks* and woven *ikats* that shimmered in the light, the Textile Room displayed a double ikat silk *patola* or wedding sari from India, where the method of weaving originated 800 years ago. Elongated diamonds enclosing birds, elephants, and flowers were typical of the *rotan chok* or jewel design of the sari. Said to be imbued with magical powers, this *patola* would have enveloped the wedding couple during the ceremony, insured continued fertility of the clan, wrapped the mother and her child when healing was needed, and covered her corpse. I especially loved all this women lore. I wondered how their men treated them. What level of independence did they enjoy? Were they allowed leadership roles in their homes and communities? Or were they satisfied simply to decorate themselves and their homes? Nowhere in the lecture notes did I find answers to those questions.

Of all the galleries, however, the one fully devoted to Indian culture and antiquities, the last one in our programmed Museum tour, was the most mysterious and fascinating to me. In the dimly lit room, we docents gathered for training with our notebooks around the temple sculptures. These were encased in clear glass showcases with ceiling spotlights lifting out of the shadows their perfect body parts nearly nude except for the jewelry. I had never before been in the presence of such sculptures—like the 13th-14th century red sandstone

Uma-Mahesvara-Marti figure from Madhya Pradesh show-ing Siva, the destroyer, one of the Hindu Triad of gods, with his voluptuous consort Paravati seated in his lap. We learned in these docent training sessions that the crossed scarf, the beaded belt, the exaggerated pelvis, and everything else we couldn't identify were most probably fertility symbols.

~

I think I must have been falling also under the spell of my new Indian friends at the Museum. I thought they were beautiful in their glittery silk saris, elegant and graceful, slyly open just at the midriff, and in the melodious way they curled their sub-continental tongues around a British accent. Laxmi, Boruna, and Maya stood out among all of us ex-pat women who made up the Friends docent core. Their lectures were the most popular. And they introduced us to Singapore's best Indian cuisine.

Along with the regular activities of lectures, field trips, and docent training, members of the Friends of the Museum hosted teas and such. Most of the ladies provided an elegant linen-tabled service with polite servings of pastry catered from European bakeries. The Indian ladies, on the other hand, put out lavish spreads, tables full of every kind of bread stacked high, *roti paratha, chapati, naan, puri, papadam* and each selected to match a complementary curry, rice, or veg-etable dish, with every sort of fresh chutney, from mango sweet, to mint and tamarind mouth-pursing sour, to fiery hot. For dessert my favorite was *gulam jamon*, sweet balls made of dried milk, flour, and cream flavored with almonds, raisins, and cardamoms, deep-fried and served in honey or sugared rose water. The sheer size of the feast reminded me of Thanksgiving at the homes of my country cousins in Virginia.

Nothing was spared in an effort to show gracious hospitality.

Divali, the Festival of Lights, India's most important holiday was an excuse for more feasting. The halls leading to our Indian friends' flats would be decked with lamps burning to lead the souls of the dead back to earth. Cliff said he thought the lights were leading us to a gastronomic paradise. Or were they leading us to a land that would change our lives forever in ways we could not then imagine?

The year I joined the Museum Friends, 1982, was memorable for Richard Attenborough's epic film of Gandhi that garnered nine academy awards. I loved the movie. I saw it the first time with Cliff and then twice more to catch what I might have missed the first time. I loved the other-worldly music, the beat of the *tabla*, the choir of men's deep voices humming that haunting refrain in G minor, the ethereal strings of Ravi Shankar's sitar playing away and away. And mainly I loved the little brown man in the loin cloth who walked with a bamboo staff, the spokesman for the conscience of all mankind. It was Einstein who is reported to have said, "Generations will scarce believe that such a one as this ever walked upon the face of the earth."

I took pen and notebook with me to the movies to record all his stirring words. "An eye for an eye only makes the whole world blind," he said. And from his bed, when he is near death from fasting in an effort to stop the violent Free India campaign marches, he said, "When I despair, I remember that all through history, the way of truth and love has always won. There have been tyrants and murderers and for a time they can seem invincible. But in the end, they always fall, always."

I traveled on the train with him wide-eyed in his discovery tour of India, that vast panorama of limitless landscapes and terrain as diverse as barren deserts, lush valleys greener than green, rice paddies, the red clay of Rajasthan. It was the most exotic land I had ever seen, peopled with great souls who were willing to be beaten to the ground in non-violent protest rather than fight back in defense of their national freedom. This was the true *e pluribus unum*. They had suffered their share of tyrants, just as we Americans had.

Something like hero-worship must have enveloped me. I was especially moved by his personal moral imperative to right the wrongs of his people, especially of the most vulnerable. I could see myself in the shoes of *Life* reporter Margaret Bourke-White taking down his every word, photographing his every move. After all, had I not been newly initiated into the journalist's fold with my recent attachment to Singapore's *Straits Times*? Investment in a camera seemed like a good idea.

When Cliff's boss suggested that India might be our next tour of duty, I was all for it. I wanted Cliff and me to experience India together for ourselves. I have to confess that at that time I was growing less enchanted with colonized Singapore, the influence of the Brits everywhere, and the pretty constant shopping hype. Singapore, for all intents and purposes, had achieved the status of the world's emporium. I was not a shopper. I was ready to move on to a less materialistic home-base.

PART II
THE CLIMB BEGINS

Chapter 4

DARJEELING

W*e reach Pema's birthplace without knowing it. We have no notion what awaits us, here on vacation to escape the intense heat of Southern India, our current home. Before we leave the States for India, my best friend Dorothy, herself a Catholic mom, says with uncanny foresight,*

"Maybe Mother Teresa has a baby for you." But the likelihood of that seems as far-fetched now as it did then. We cannot have anticipated either the baby or the size of the mountain we have to climb, if we have any hope of adopting her.

~

Our climb began in a restaurant near the roof of the world —Darjeeling, famous for its tea plantations and favored by the British colonials as a hill station providing rest and relief from the intense heat of the plains below. Nestled in the Himalayan foothills, on a clear day Darjeeling commands a spectacular view of Mount Kanchenjunga's jagged peaks, at 8598 meters the third highest mountain in the world on the border between Nepal and Sikkim. The tiny mountain kingdom of Sikkim had become an Indian protectorate and originally included Darjeeling, which the King of Sikkim had

granted to the British for use as a hill station. This is where
the Viceroy and his retinue would settle in during the four
hottest months of the year to decorate the State houses with
their full-dress uniformed fetes and fancy balls.

Our less formal gathering marked a reunion of old friends
from Singapore. They had just arrived in Darjeeling toward
the end of November 1984 on the last leg of a week-long
pilgrimage to Bhutan. Cliff and I were on R&R from Bangalore, our company posting in south India. Local Tibetans
helped fill up the long table at The Snow Lion. Everywhere
you looked, the walls were decorated with old hunting prints.
The ancient waiters, stooped and wizened, looked to be of
the same British Raj era, complete with white gloves. The
Tibetans were close friends of the group's anointed leader,
Jane Perkins, who was my editor at Singapore's *Straits Times*
and also a close personal friend.

On my left sat Pema, a lovely Tibetan woman, whose arts
and crafts shop was known to be the most authentic and
popular among foreign tourists. She noticed that there were
children present but none of them mine. Since arriving in
Asia three years earlier, we had been the object of pity by all
our Asian friends because we were childless. Cliff's clients
had taken to giving us gifts of fertility symbols, an especially
memorable one from Papua New Guinea that would have
scared the stork away. It was like a giant lollipop with pukka
shells for eyes and the neck embedded in a very sharp-pointed
crescent moon. The gifts didn't stop there. Once over beer and
nasi padang with his Indonesian counterpart, Cliff had been
offered a second wife, only for the purpose of childbearing,
of course.

Here in India, as in most of Asia, your value as a woman

was gauged by how many children you could produce. A well-meaning Sikh lady told me that I would never truly be "grown up" until I had a child of my own, which was only a matter of stimulating certain dormant hormones. Yoga, she said, would take care of that nicely. Yoga does nice things for my body but I don't know about the hormones. Frankly, I had never thought of motherhood as defining my womanhood, until now.

"Did your children not join you?" Pema asked.

"No, we have no children. Yet," I answered politely. I figured she did not want to hear how Cliff and I had been working diligently with one of Singapore's foremost fertility specialists, and how it seemed we might be making some progress in spite of Cliff's constant trips out of Singapore and unpredictable travel schedule when suddenly we were posted to India.

Dr. Ong must have been a Sumo wrestler in another life. Every time she examined me with her tough, icy hands, I came away feeling like something between a grinding stone and a chopping block. I had been poked and prodded, D & Cd, and laparoscopied to the point where I felt more specimen than human. Anyway, she discovered that I had not been ovulating after all these years of menstruation. The curse had been arriving regular as clockwork and so excruciating I wanted to rip out the whole baby-making apparatus.

"Ovaries smooth as porcelain," the doctor announced after the last of the exploratory surgeries. I had this picture of my womb shaped like a blue and white Ming vase and just as cold and empty. She told me not to worry, that she wanted me to take Clomid and then some injection that promised wondrous results before we moved into in-vitro fertilization.

I missed the miracle drug because we had to leave Singapore

for India. It was rumored that Indian medicine was risky, at best. Still I had hope, since one of my good friends even older than I, that is, on the other side of 40, had just had a healthy first baby.

"It nearly killed me," Peggy wrote. She was still recovering a year later.

Back in March, just a few months after our arrival in India, I shared my baby thoughts with my best friend Dorothy in Dubuque, Iowa. I was answering her letter announcing that my first husband and his new wife were about to have a baby.

It may come as no surprise to you if I say that truthfully I've never wanted a baby desperately, the way I hear it from other women. And I'm trying now to believe that my lack of inspiration toward motherhood isn't so abnormal or makes of me some kind of freak or less a loving and lovable person, woman. I'm always glad for others when a baby comes into their lives and I'm pleased for my former husband. But I've never been particularly interested in being around babies and I wonder how Cliff's well-ordered, pack-rat universe would survive them. I don't think I am any less attuned to cosmic rhythms simply because my biological processes haven't performed the miracle of a baby. I think that's a reference to my hero Germaine Greer. According to Hindu beliefs, I am told, I will not reach heaven unless I produce a son.

~

"Had you thought about adopting?" Pema asked, back at the restaurant.

"Well, yes, sort of." I did not want to give the impression that we were actively searching, but then I was not opposed to the idea either. "As a matter of fact, a baby was offered to us as recently as last month in Bangalore. You know, way

View of Mt. Kanchenjunga from Darjeeling

down south and west of Madras. That's where we live now."

"And it didn't work out?"

"No, a very nice woman came to us representing the family of the baby. She told us that they had too many children. They couldn't afford to feed them all. And would we be interested in adopting her."

"What did you say?"

"I was entertaining the idea, even though Cliff was on the road and I had no way of reaching him. She was a beautiful little Tamil baby and felt so comfortable in my arms. But the very same day her parents came from Andhra Pradesh and fetched her. They were very apologetic. They said they could not give her up."

"Oh, Tamil, very dark then." At that puzzling remark, I was reluctant to share more information. I have to admit that I was surprised by what felt like "mothering instincts" when I held that four-month-old baby in my arms.

Cliff's view was practical and cautious, as always. We must find out the requirements for adoption, all the legal ramifications, discuss with this one and that, what are the costs, will the parents come after us for extortion or whatever. He always looked at things from that angle—the worst that could happen. But I have learned to appreciate his carefulness. If not this baby then another, I said to myself.

My mind shifted from our conversation to the layers of jewelry Pema, the shop keeper, was wearing, all traditional Tibetan, fat beads of coral and turquoise strung round her neck and woven in the braid that crowned her head. At the end of a beaded garland, a square silver amulet in the shape of a box rested on her chest. It was large enough to bait my curiosity as to its contents. Although I was tempted, I didn't ask. To my mind, we had already ended the conversation.

"Come with me tomorrow early," she said, to my surprise. "I have a place in mind I want you to visit. We'll have to do some climbing, so be sure to wear your comfortable shoes." Not wanting to seem rude, I gave a nod to her plan.

Next morning early, all the women in our group gathered at the Windamere Hotel patio for the visit to wherever. Jane had organized her Bhutan trek to include two of her *Straits Times* staff members, Muriel and Linda with her two children, plus her old friend Gael and former husband Phil from Australia. I was glad to see Chuni join the group of women, too. Jane had taken the young Tibetan woman under her wing some years ago when Chuni was a child and both of them new to Darjeeling.

Word had gone around that we were going to look at babies. In spite of the monsoon season, the November day shone crisp and clear, and I could see why the locals called

Kanchenjunga the "queen of mountains." Pema took the lead.

"We're going to Mother Teresa's house," she said.

"Oh, yes," Jane chimed in. "That's right. She has an orphanage here somewhere." Like good schoolgirls on a field trip, we followed Pema down ribbons of narrow streets that now and then broke into steep stairways. We passed blocks of pastel-colored buildings made of wood that looked to be stacked on one another, old and new chock-a-block with flat rusty tin roof-tops, balconies, and abundant windows opening to the breathtaking mountain panorama. Then we abruptly turned to the right and were climbing, climbing ever upward toward a place Pema's finger was pointing at the very top of the hill. For some reason, I wasn't bothered by the difficulty of the climb. It must have been the effects of the altitude. I was giddy with the whole adventure.

A group of what looked to be local women and girls of every Himalayan shape and hue—Lepsha or Bhutia from Sikkim, Nepali, West Bengali Indian, all from Darjeeling's melting pot—greeted us at the courtyard entrance to Shanta Bhawan, the name designating Mother Teresa's orphanages in this region. This low-slung group of connected buildings that looked like a school compound had been turned into a safe haven for Mother Teresa's Missionaries of Charity work on behalf of children, the sick, and dying. Two of the workers, an older woman and a young girl in black braids, immediately broke from the group and then returned with a tiny bundle. It was a boy, which they displayed with great pride. I wasn't surprised since I knew by now how much Asians preferred boys.

For some reason, I was drawn to the crib in the corner of the large room, dark except for the one window admitting

Bonnie holding baby Pema with M.C. helper
at Shanti Bhavan, Darjeeling

light. "May I see this baby?" I asked. With some hesitation, the older woman went over to the crib, reached in and brought out the baby, a girl. Cliff and I had talked about our preference for a girl.

Now the expedition seemed less like a baby shopping trip and more like destiny. All of us went out into the light of the courtyard to see the baby. While I was doing my best to cradle the newborn properly, my heart sank when I saw the dark blue charcoal coloring on her forehead. This was repeated round her tiny wrists and ankles. I thought that these must be bruises and that somebody had abused this baby.

Chuni, who was trained as a nurse, gathered up the baby and her blankets like a pro and announced without having been asked, "She's a healthy baby girl." As it turned out, the ash spread across her forehead was a local home-grown cure for warding off all forms of disease brought on by the mountain cold, including tuberculosis. Still I wondered and worried about those bruises on her wrists and ankles. Chuni explained these away as Mongolian spots or birthmarks commonly seen on babies and children up to the age of four in this region, in China and all of Asia. Nevertheless I was not convinced. I had to fight the compulsion to bundle her up in my arms and take her home with me.

Returning back down the hill and all the way to the Windamere, I was still feeling the warmth of the baby and looking into that exotic little face surrounded by the planet's tallest mountain peaks. In this faraway place, I heard the words of a little poem I'd written 10 years ago. At the time, to suppress my failing marriage, I was focused on that ten-acre piece of Illinois farmland on Sugar Creek and what I had hoped to grow on it.

> *One violet hidden in a patch of grass*
> *has the power of a camera flash*
> *to catch the eye and strip it bare*
> *to spread violets everywhere.*

Chapter 5

HOW HIGH THE MOUNTAIN?

I*n the downhill walk with the women clustered around me, cheering me on, all I can see is that tiny bundle of baby girl. We can have our baby! Whatever doubts I have about how I would adjust to such a small one are dispelled in those moments I am holding her, rocking us into comfort together. My vision of the world is different. It will never be quite the same, whatever the outcome. I want to write to my mother, to Cliff's mother, to best friend Dorothy, to all my sympathetic women friends, to everyone, some kind of announcement, a birth or rebirth, is it? Now to convince Cliff.*

~

On our return to the Windamere, I found Cliff with the men in the group waiting lunch for us. It was hard, but I tried to contain my excitement over the miracle of what had just happened. After all, there were so many questions. Was Cliff ready for such an undertaking? Certainly we wanted children but up until recently expected to have our own. Was he willing to adopt a baby? Was he willing to adopt a foreign baby? Was the baby even available to us? How complicated would adopting her be? I think I was trying to prepare myself for the worst.

Both of us would have so many adjustments to make and over an indefinitely long period of time. Here in India his patience seemed to be thinning even more, so I could not imagine how he would react to the inconveniences of a baby. I knew the childcare responsibilities would be largely mine. It could be the most fulfilling experience of my life (they say), or the most exhausting at my age. And unless we should adopt, I would have to face long, complicated experiments with this dose of hormones and that injection, timed just at the right hour and in which part of the world. Also I remember certain phases in my life when I had a tendency to take on more responsibility than I could handle. Would I see that ugly face in the mirror again? I would be caring not only for our adopted daughter but also for the child of the birth mother. I owed it to her to be the best mother I could be. I owed it to her to be the perfect mother.

Then factor in agent-orange. Cliff knew he had been exposed to the deadly chemical. The poisoned jungles and waterways he and his platoon waded through in Vietnam in early 1968 were evidence enough. The men filled their canteens and drank the water from the rivers and streams when they were on long-range recon patrol. Frequently we heard news of too many Vietnamese children born with disabilities. Now we were hearing the same heart-breaking news about the children of Vietnam veterans. Cliff left the service with a mouth sore that developed into cancer and resulted in the loss of bone and three teeth from his upper left jaw. But typically, rather than dwell on his war experience, he would make light of our baby-making situation.

"Suppose we had a baby. Just imagine what it would look like with our joint DNA—another short book end with piano legs, all calf and no ankle." I could imagine a boy surviving that well enough with a future in football or wrestling, but God bless the girl-child with piano legs. Even though the Women's Movement was in full force by now, anatomy was still destiny. What would be the future prospects for our natural daughter?

"Well, if Bonnie and Cliff won't have her, I will," said Gael rather emphatically from the next table. Gael already had one son, as golden blond as she was. Although now divorced from his father Phil, she and Phil were together more or less as a couple on the Bhutan trip. I really did not take her seriously, but it seemed urgent to get Cliff to the orphanage as soon as we could get there. I tried my best to describe her tiny face and the marks I had seen and the experience of the orphanage to pique his curiosity, but we decided to let his lunch settle first.

By late afternoon Cliff and I together made the climb to Shanta Bhawan. As soon as we entered the courtyard, the girl in black braids ran into the office without a word to us. Always on the look-out for antique vehicles, Cliff's attention immediately turned to the small shed that served as a garage next to the office. Here a retired Gurkha was hanging a 60-watt light bulb over the fuel filter of a jeep to warm the diesel overnight, he told Cliff. The nuns used the old Mahindra, modeled on a 1950s Jeep, to deliver medicines every morning around Darjeeling.

We turned to find the nun in charge, Sister Jean, there to greet us. A prospective father making his appearance seemed to give the enterprise more weight.

Jane and Amala in Darjeeling

"You've come to see your daughter," she said to Cliff, who wasn't agreeing to anything just yet, still trying to catch his breath after the climb. As soon as he laid eyes on the baby girl, however, he was totally smitten. I patiently waited for my turn to hold her, but he wasn't letting go.

"I just want to see her open her eyes. Come to think of it, I've rarely held a baby," he said, cradling her closer. Taking account of his reaction with great satisfaction, the smiling Sister presented the beginning steps necessary to adopt her. First we should know that eventually she would be taken down the mountain to Tindharia, some 50 km to the south. There the climate was more gentle and she would be safe from tuberculosis. Sister Dionysia had charge of the M.C. orphanage there. It would be a good idea if we met her as soon as possible. As far as the history of the baby was concerned, the known facts were these, according to Sister Jean. She was approximately ten days old. She was born in Victoria Hospital there in Darjeeling. The mother had left the hospital after giving birth to the baby, who was now officially considered abandoned. In cases such as this, babies were turned over to the care of Mother Teresa's orphanage.

So, without a look backward, we hired a car, India's trademark Ambassador. Tank-like in its demeanor, it promised protection if not comfort on the road we were about to travel. True to its name, the Hill Cart road to and from Darjeeling had not been much improved since being laid out in the early 19th century to accommodate travel by bullock cart. No matter. After Sister Jean's whispered word to the driver, we were hell-bent for Tindharia and Sister Dionysia down the one-lane, impassable road, clinging to the side of the mountain around hair-pin curves above many a breathtaking abyss, the driver honking at every blind spot to announce our approach and avoid a collision.

We passed the Darjeeling Himalayan Railway, affectionately known as the "toy train," chugging up the hill, just two cars behind an ancient steam engine. I remembered hearing somewhere that this was Mother Teresa's way of passage to and from Darjeeling in those early years of her novitiate teaching at the Loreto Convent School in Darjeeling and then as a professed nun traveling the last leg from Calcutta 400 miles away. I imagined her sitting in prayer fingering her rosary on one of those cold metal seats on 10 September 1946. She was headed for her retreat in Darjeeling and is said to have heard Jesus' call to serve Him in the slums of Calcutta's poorest of the poor. Four years later she would have the new congregation she dreamed of, the Missionaries of Charity.

~

Sister Dionysia, the nun originally from Kerala State in Mother Teresa's service, had her hands full in Tindharia. The property she had been given to transform into an orphanage was an old crumbling mansion with tea estate and a history. India's most famous poet Rabindranath Tagore had been a frequent family guest during the early part of the century. The Sister was just in process of waving off a visiting group of Belgian doctors and instructing the workmen who were renovating one of the out-buildings to function as a kitchen. Abruptly, she discharged them all as soon as she saw us.

For some reason, the bespectacled nun immediately took a liking to Cliff. Perhaps she recognized the farm boy in him, or the altar-boy-turned-lapsed-Catholic. In white cotton sari covering her forehead with the signature blue stripes, she pulled on a pair of muddy boots and handed us each a bucket.

"I want you to see the work we're doing to fix up the place before winter comes. We have to get the babies from Darjeeling here as soon as we can," she said. On our tour of the estate, she pointed out the planting she had already undertaken to feed the children and staff. Colorful fat squashes and pumpkin, fledgling banana trees, kale and leafy dark greens, eggplant, broad beans, okra, and red onions spread in patches up the hillside. With our buckets full of vegetables, we finished the tour at the hilltop gazebo where Tagore was said to have composed some of his most popular poems.

Back down the hill, she showed us where the children lived and where our baby would come to live in a wide-open space filled with cribs and children of various sizes. She gave us lunch with her staff, a congenial mix of nuns and laywomen smiling and laughing shoulder to shoulder in some kind of joyfully spiritual conspiracy. The event ended in singing and prayers for us in our tender mission. Then she escorted us to the tiny chapel and sat us down.

"I am sorry to have to tell you that the baby you love has already been spoken for. Babies in the care of Mother Teresa's order, Missionaries of Charity, in this region are destined for Belgium." I wanted to protest as loud as I could that surely we did not come all this way to find out that the baby we had just seen and loved could not be ours. Something in her eyes, however, kept me silent. She would do what she could to help us, but we really needed to visit Sister Margaret Mary, the nun in charge of M.C. adoptions. She was the one we would have to persuade. We would find her located at the Motherhouse in Calcutta. Then Sister Dionysia motioned toward the words printed on the white wall over the altar.

Everything is grace for everything is God's gift.
Whatever be the character of life or its unexpected events,
To the heart that loves, all is well.
                                        St. Therese of Lisieux

"You must carry these words in your hearts," she said to my eyes brimming with tears. "We will do all we can on this end. Now with God's grace it is up to you to do what you can. I must tell you that in this line of work we have come to believe in miracles."

I'm not sure how carefully we were listening or how much she wanted us to understand. It was clear to both of us that Sister Dionysia was favoring us for the baby's adoptive parents. Never mind the prior commitment to Belgium. I suppose we should have asked right then and there what we needed to do precisely, what steps we should take in what order. We must have been caught up in that moment, under the spell of Sister Dionysia in her white sari. Or was it the holiness of that place with its rough plastered walls empty of furnishings except the altar bearing the limp body of Jesus on a wooden cross? But off we went inspired by the Sister's confidence in us to do what we had to do to adopt this baby.

Chapter 6

THE MYSTERY BABY

B*y now it is clear that we cannot just bundle up the baby and take off with her. In his frustration at the Church bureaucracy, the soldier-side of Cliff is making noises that way. But I know that absconding with her would be totally out of the question. We have to follow whatever rules are laid out to us in Calcutta and move in the Indian way, slow and tedious as I have come to know that is.*

~

That night, back in Darjeeling, the Singapore group gathered at Amala's place in the Tibetan enclave. Amala and her daughters, Chuni and teen-aged Yeshi, had become like family to Jane some years ago when Jane befriended them, fresh refugees selling used clothing in a market stall on Nehru Road, the main shopping street. Amala's cozy one-room floor-to-ceiling living/storage reminded me of Mole's underground nest in Kenneth Grahame's *Wind in the Willows*. She warmed us with *chang*, her home-brew made of millet, and floor-to-wall carpets in thick wool, primary colors, and simple patterns typical of Tibetan weaving. Although we could barely understand each other, she seemed to want me to know that she was there for me.

She took my hand and drew me beside her on her couch.

"Amala," I remember whispering in her ear, trying to keep it simple and unobtrusive so as not to draw attention to myself. "I've never had such feelings for a child, and I don't know how to explain them, my feelings. This business of motherhood is so new and scary. I'm not sure if I am capable or ready for the responsibility. I'm just over 40, and I should be ready! She would not be just mine and Cliff's baby but she has another mother, her birth mother. So I would also be responsible for another woman's child. Do you see what I am saying?" Amala smiled and nodded and moved even closer. " It feels like the most important decision of my life, and we're not at all sure we can have her. It's all up to somebody in Calcutta. My hopes and dreams all hinge on some stranger's permission. Does any of this make sense, Amala?" She just held my hand and smiled and nodded as if her heart understood everything I was saying.

Everyone in the room was speculating about the baby's birth parents. Everyone had an opinion, everyone familiar enough with the region and the features of the mountain tribal groups. "Well, she can't be Tibetan," said Gael flatly. "We all know how the Tibetans take care of their own. Especially if the mother were Tibetan, they would be looking after her at the Tibetan Refugee Self-Help Centre." Amala appeared to agree with this view. Her daughter Yeshi seemed a little skeptical.

"But she looks Tibetan," said Phil, Gael's ex-husband, gesturing with his mug of brew. "Hell, she could even pass for Hawaiian or Japanese!"

"That's it," said Linda. "Her features could match any of these Mongolian racial groups. They are so similar. She could be Lepcha or Bhutia from Sikkim, or Nepali or Tibetan. Let's see if they put the red *tikka* dot on her forehead. That will be the telling clue. The *tikka* would say she is Hindu, maybe Nepali."

"We have to consider where she was born," said Jane, waiting until everyone had voiced an opinion. "Who can afford to deliver a baby at Victoria Hospital? My guess is that one of the wealthy girls from Sikkim at Loretto College got into trouble. The father paid for the hospitalization, and the daughter made her escape, for whatever reasons. If you know the story of Mother Teresa, you would remember that Mother came to Loretto as a girl herself. That was her first assignment when she came to India."

"I want to see your baby," Yeshi whispered to me, taking the empty place next to me on Amala's couch. She seemed to know something. Perhaps the father was Tibetan? But we never learned what information she might have had. Perhaps she was not at liberty to share it.

~

Discussion of Sikkim reminded me of Hope Cooke and the most famous, uniquely American romance of my college years. All my late-to-marry sorority sisters identified with Hope. They were holding out for "the prince," one as mature and handsome as the prince from the tiny mountain kingdom of Sikkim—land of red pandas, snow lions, cardamom plantations, and hundreds of native orchid species growing wild in its emerald-green, forested Shangri La.

I knew their story well from newspapers and fashion

magazines. I could not believe my good fortune in having landed in this once unimaginably mysterious land. How could this be? My young girl's fascination with their story so long ago was playing out now in my own imagined "romance." If I stepped inside it, their history and my even tenuous connection with it some 20 years before the baby appeared in my life felt like more than coincidence. Had I been unconsciously drawn to this region because of memories past?

Hope and the prince, soon-to-be king, had met and fallen in love right here at the Windamere Hotel, the very same hotel where we were staying. She was an orphaned debutante from Sarah Lawrence on a spiritual tour of India, and he, a lonely widower twice her age with two children. As the fairy tale goes, they immediately recognized and sympathized with each other's isolation, and he proposed on their second date. Hope became the *Gyalmo* (Queen consort) of Palden Thondrup Nangyal, the 12th *Chogyal* (King) of Sikkim in 1963. *National Geographic* covered the wedding, and *The New Yorker* followed them on a visit to the States.

Eleven years later, politics interfered in their happy-ever-after. On the death of Nehru, who had respected the independence of Sikkim and its enlightened leader, Sikkim lost its separate status. Hope's husband the King was put under house arrest in 1975. New to the job of Prime Minister, Indira Gandhi was simply responding to the noisy majority influx of Hindu Gurkhas from Nepal who had taken over the country. Once a buffer zone between Bhutan, Nepal, and Chinese-communist-occupied Tibet, Sikkim's territory was annexed as far as Darjeeling and became the 26th Indian state.

Hope and the children, both his children by his first wife and her two children by him, bowed to their father, touched

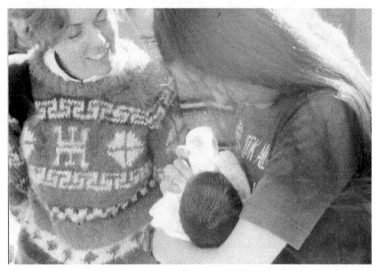

Bonnie, baby Pema, and Chuni

forehead-to-forehead in the Buddhist family tradition, and flew to New York where they settled. Hope and the King were divorced and shortly thereafter he died of cancer in New York.

Sikkim had such a checkered history of peoples of identical racial ties infiltrating its borders for over 500 years, peacefully and otherwise. The earliest settlers were the Lepchas, spirit-worshipers from Assam followed by the Bhutias and other Buddhist sects from Tibet, and the Ghurkas from Nepal. West Bengali Indians were the last arrivals.

To theorize that the baby was "Sikkimese" was simply begging the question. Cliff and I decided that it really didn't matter about her roots or why the mother had abandoned her. In the baby's disfavor was the fact that she was not a boy and she had extensive smoke-colored birth-marks on her arms, legs, and up her back, all of which made us love her even more.

She was a mountain baby and that was that. No, just by

looking at her you could see that she in herself bore all the attributes of a tiny mountain kingdom.

Out of curiosity, Cliff and I hired an open-air jeep to take us to Sikkim. Dark green clumps of tea shrubs with buttery blossoms edged the zig-zag trail. Goats and chickens scurried out of our way. At the very edge of the one-horse trail, the mountain dove deep below to the Teesta River that bordered Sikkim and our destination. When we reached the River, we were told we could go no further. We didn't have the requisite permission to cross the border. Usually it took six weeks after you made application, according to Tombo, our Sherpa guide. Besides, a lot of military police were patrolling the area and he didn't want to tangle with them.

We stopped at the bottom of the hill. Tombo parked our jeep in what looked like a ghost-town. He led us through an alleyway behind a few village huts and overgrown gardens of millet, kale, chilies, papaya trees, and thin stalks of corn. Forked palms growing from the mountainside dipped streamer tresses toward the river rushing blue-green and clear golden across pale gray sand and rock. Where the sun struck, it made the sand a gray glitter and warmed my face and the top of my head. We saw a boy with the coloring and shape of our baby's face lightly skipping over the rocks singing a song and carrying a heavy burden strapped to his head. Cliff motioned toward the women and men washing clothes in tin pans on top of boulders on the Sikkim side. Again the similarity to the baby was strong.

I got down on my knees at the river's edge and selected one of the many stones that had specks of mica. On one side of the stone's sparkling gray surface, you could make out a female image, like a little girl, depending on how you turned it. And the stone fit nicely in my cupped hand. If I couldn't have the baby just yet, at least I could have something of her supposed native land, some small talisman to wish on.

Interlude

IN THE HIMALAYAN ZOO, DARJEELING

I kept looking for my exit
past the caged cheetahs
soft-padding cell floors, back
and forth, locked in their panicky eyes
until I saw a crumbling stair
cut through a ferny dell,
a wall and the open sky beyond.

I climbed over the locked gate
and touched down
on the other side
a narrow ledge evenly tread
and the deep green valley below
like a well I could see the future
far flung over tea terraces
dropping down and down.

Coming on evening,
not knowing how far I'd come
or how many miles back
to the circle of friends by the fire
I kept to the forest path
the oaks twined and looping creepers
great secrets hidden in their cups
and the perfect ferns formed a curtain
close as my right shoulder
rustling with night creatures.

The switchback path
like a loose string
wound round the mountain
leading always away
to those impossible peaks
reached only by a few
and after so many turns
meeting no one but myself
all hope of direction lost
I climbed for freedom
believing each tree and rock
and tiny mountain kingdom
knew the way.

Chapter 7
AT HOME IN BANGALORE

Before we can arrange that fateful meeting with Sister Margaret Mary at the Calcutta Motherhouse, we begin to explore all we need to do to speed up the adoption process. Cliff arranges his work schedule so that he can include visits with Pema in the Tindharia orphanage. As much as we want her with us, she is probably safer there.

~

To adopt a baby you find a lawyer who specializes in adoptions. Right? Wrong. In India, where there were very few foreigners living at that time due to the ban on new Christian missionaries, there was no business in foreign adoptions. Most adoptions were carried on from overseas by adoptive parents living in Europe or the States, if not locally by mostly Hindu families according to Indian federal law. Hindus had the first choice of India's abandoned babies, favoring boys over girls. In part, we were at a disadvantage because we were resident in India because of Cliff's work there. I failed to understand how long-distance parents, sight-unseen, were preferable to ones ready-made on Indian soil.

At this point in November 1984, we had been living in

the south of India, in Karnataka state's capital city Bangalore since our posting there less than a year earlier from Singapore. Cliff was the resident manager in all of India for an American firm called Haulpak out of Peoria, Illinois. He was known as a self-styled country boy with a Master's in fixing anything in a country where nothing worked and nobody cared. He was also known as an invaluable source of information about remote places throughout Asia where he was free to go and others were not. Haulpak was in the business of supplying the world's mining industry with earth-moving machines that rolled on tires taller than most basketball players. The company was under contract to Bharat Ltd. Earth Movers, a military defense operation under the Indian government.

When we had arrived early in 1984, the commercial attaché in Madras told us that there were now only 25 American business people resident in all of India. The other Americans were either journalists on temporary visas or spouses of Indians. According to the unofficial limit placed on resident visas, we were replacing the gentleman who had just brushed past us in the steamy hallway. He looked none too happy about the failure of his visa to be renewed .

"Company in-fighting over the quality of maintenance," the attaché said under his breath, staring into the bundle of yellowing papers tied up in red string. "Had only two years left to retirement. He was planning to retire here in India, too."

"Which company?" Cliff asked.

"Union Carbide."

Union Carbide made front-page news less than a year later. On the night of December 2-3, 1984, just a month after Pema's birth (as best we could calculate), the Bhopal factory in the state of Madhya Pradesh producing the pesticide Sevin leaked gas that is said to have killed over 25,000 people in the final tally. The cause was attributed to poor maintenance.

I have no idea how it happened, but it looked like we had landed in India during one of its most volatile periods of twentieth-century history. Less than a week before Pema's birth (as best we could calculate), India's Prime Minister Indira Gandhi was assassinated by her Sikh body guards. We were shocked but not surprised. Her assassination seemed like the last stroke in over a year full of senseless violence that seemed unending.

Following her assassination, terrible reprisals and increasing turmoil in the Sikh-dominated Punjab region dominated the news. Angry scores continued to be settled in the most brutal ways. The colleague waiting to meet Cliff in Delhi had been confined to his hotel for a week while riots and civil unrest plagued the city. From his window he watched a mob drag a Sikh from his home and beat him to death in the street. But the "Big Elephant" kept lumbering along, while we waited to see if Rajiv would inherit his mother's enemies and her dictatorial habits. With all the rumors about a CIA plot, Americans weren't very popular.

Cliff postponed that trip to Delhi until the rage cooled. I was hoping he would stay home, shave off his beard, something. But the Company was calling and we could not hold out inside our house forever. Bangalore seemed safe enough, although worriers told us to stay off the streets and out of the way of stones. Finally I was allowed to do my marketing, went to yoga class, all the routine stuff escorted by Cliff's body guard and driver, ex-Subedhar Major Muthuswami, formerly of the Madras Sappers Regiment (engineering unit). It was a relief to get out of the house, even if I wasn't allowed to drive the car myself. Even though I had an international driver's license issued in Singapore, the company had decided in its wisdom that damages would be so extreme, should I hit a pedestrian or a sacred cow, we were all safer if I were not behind the wheel.

In the matter of safety, I should also mention the spate of communal disturbances practically at our front door. Soon after we had unpacked, we were house-bound for over one week while the police tried to deal with the rioting and bus burnings that spread from the old bazaar to the city. Our next-door neighbor Kavery took us to see one of the buses before it was towed away.

"I know it is hard to believe," she said, "but we Indians are truly peace-loving people. When this sort of thing happens, we are always surprised and shocked."

The violence finally came to a halt when the police shot randomly into a crowd protesting a Tamil movie and three people were killed—all over language. It seems the British had established state boundaries back during Partition ostensibly along language lines. All signs, documents, even movie theatres in Bangalore, as the capital of Karnataka State, were supposed to be in the state language, Kanada. However Tamil had gradually superseded Kanada with the majority population influx of Tamil-speaking people. Kanadans felt disenfranchised. While the police were fighting the fires, city maintenance crews went to work white-washing all the tombstone-shaped street signs. They repainted the signs in Kanada and then when tempers had cooled added English and finally Tamil.

My energy had remained consistently high since home-leave in July, except for spells when Cliff returned from two

From left, Chuni, cousin Phurbu Lhamu, and Yeshi

weeks away and I lapsed into laziness, fussing in the kitchen, house-bound stuff that turned into duty and then resentment. I longed for his company and worried about him when he was away for these long stretches. I was relieved to see him when he arrived home and then relieved when he returned to the road, so that I could find my writing routine again. What a crazy life we lived. Once I had this dream of being blown out of a cannon.

Although I lived in hopes of words spilling out of me like the Ganges, I could report that since end July, I had sent some seven poems (revised and new) by request for submission to an Illinois anthology-in-the-works and drafted a 5,000-word promotional piece for a sculptor-friend in Iowa. Word came from Singapore that *Singapore Green*, my Botanic Gardens book published last year, had won the best book-design award in Singapore, and I was receiving fan mail all the way from Botswana!

MY FORTUNE

I feel my fortune in bits of string,
newspapers and empty glass jars,
the light spilling reckless over the wall,
the bougainvillea and stalky cannas—
in everything that wants pruning.
The rag picker's eyes covet
even my shredded poems;
in her watch, nothing is wasted
not an eggshell or an onion peel.
I imagine she gathers to herself
all these discarded parts of my days
mixing what was used well
with what was not,
and bears them in her sack
through rivers of men and buffalo
far away to an earthen floor.
In shadows from an oil lamp,
a small dog curls at her feet
and all I've shed empties into her lap
a fluttering avalanche of paper,
hairpins, pencil stubs, dried tuber
roses, and red cigarette boxes,
the wealth of maharanis. Mustard oil
shines on her hair, on her fingers,
her nimble brown fingers as they
piece together garments like jewel-
eyed peacock feathers unfolding
warm shawls for the children,
garlands for the elephant god
and for her ears, studs
of silver and crystal and diamond.

Chapter 8

THE POLITICS OF VIOLENCE

The level of communal turmoil in India is growing weekly, if not day-by-day. 1984, the year of our daughter's birth, marks the advent of a long period of unrest and physical danger. The threatening atmosphere that is becoming a regular part of our life in Bangalore has the effect of reducing the urgency to push through the adoption.

~

We had arrived in India at the tail-end of the "New India" and Congress (I) party rule under Indira Gandhi. The "I" stood for Indira, a dominant political force in India since 1959 and Prime Minister-elect three times over. She was an iconic figure, unmistakable in a crowd with her electric shock of white hair and "20th century Mona Lisa smile," that meant all things to all men according to the *Chicago Times*, —probably a reference to her ability to charm both Richard Nixon and Leonid Brezhnev in visits less than two months apart.

Mrs. Gandhi ruled her democracy with an iron fist deploying military troops now to quell the rising communal violence. These early eighties were hard times even by Indian standards.

The fledgling democracy had endured and survived the Emergency in 1975 when she became a virtual dictator. In response
to the political unrest, strikes, boycotts, and demonstrations
opposing her party, she had suspended all civil liberties,
banned opposition political parties, enforced tough press
censorship and had thousands of political opponents arrested
and jailed. These stop-gap methods lasted almost two years
until she and her Congress party were defeated in the national
elections by the Janata Party.

Indira had originally groomed her youngest son Sanjay to
replace her and continue the Nehru dynasty. In his efforts to
implement the Emergency in 1975-76, Sanjay had taken it
upon himself to "beautify" India's capital city by demolishing
miles of Old Mughal Delhi's shacks, shops, and residences
that were home and livelihood to half a million Muslims.
These were squatter settlements peopled by wave after wave
of impoverished farm families who could not survive on the
land. They constructed by hand row upon row of make-shift,
tin-roofed huts crowded together down narrow zigzag lanes
with doors of plywood and thin, shared walls.

Then to help curtail India's growing population, Sanjay
enthusiastically campaigned for sterilization of all men who
had more than two children. To meet the high targeted numbers, the police forcibly rounded up mainly the poor and
defenseless. Sanjay managed to alienate his mother's strongest
supporters, the Muslims and the poor. Unwittingly he helped
bring about her defeat in the 1977 election she decided to
hold to legitimize her emergency regime. He was well on
his way to the top of the political arena, until he attempted
the reckless airplane stunt that took his life.

~

In actual fact, we Americans were not particularly welcome in India as far as either the Janata or Congress party was concerned. Both the socialist left and the Hindu right were suspicious of all capitalists believing them to be greedy and self-serving. Indian politicians of all stripes were determined to keep India safe from American culture and material goods. Their plan was to take the money for wheat subsidies, thank you, and then run the helping agencies off. They got rid of the Peace Corps and nationalized Coca Cola, IBM, and all the oil companies. Gas cylinders came at a premium. If we managed to get one, we had to pay more than the locals. Since the power in Bangalore was shut off to all residential customers at 6:30 a.m., I boiled water every night and stored it in thermoses for the morning coffee. Sometimes we had to siphon gas out of Cliff's Enfield motorcycle to fire up our mountain stove.

After her reelection in 1980 at an energetic age 62, Mrs. Gandhi was faced with provincial unrest in the north-eastern tribal states aiming at separation. One of the Indian government's most serious problems since Independence had been the vast regional discrepancies in terms of standard of living—comparatively high in the western states, and to the north, poor, rural, and overpopulated. These differences provided a fermenting ground for separatist movements.

On top of that, the Russian invasion of Afghanistan, 86,000 troops strong, was threatening her borders. The Islamic Republic of Pakistan was moving toward its fellow Muslim nations in the Middle East and away from reunification with India. Not only that, Indira was facing an opposition faction in the Punjab seeking separation to create its own "Nation"—this her most prosperous state, the tiny Punjab, home to Sikhs, India's fourth largest religious group, distinctive for their beards and turbans and military prowess. Their elite Sikh regiment formed the backbone of India's army and provided recruits for her personal bodyguards.

The violent reaction came to a head when a militant Sikh faction demanded complete independence for the Punjab and creation of a new Sikh state. They openly defied the government and sent out motorcycle gangs to terrorize the countryside. Indira waited for moderation to prevail. When it did not, she launched Operation Blue Star.

On the night of June 5, 1984 she ordered Indian army commandos to storm the Sikh holdout—their most revered shrine, the Mecca of the Sikh faith, The Golden Temple at Amritsar. By the next day, when most of the leadership had been rounded up and dispatched, thousands of Sikhs lay dead on the desecrated Temple grounds. Their irreplaceable library of ancient Sikh religious scripture was destroyed. The secessionist leader Jarnail Singh Bhindranwale was made a martyr. The idea of a separate Sikh state grew stronger than ever, now that it was clear that Indira's regime could not be trusted. Her Congress (I) party looked just like the other oppressors in India's history to the now deeply alienated Sikh community.

At this time, Cliff was on assignment at the Kolar Gold Fields about 100 km east of Bangalore, which was far to the south nearly a subcontinent away from Delhi and the Punjab, far from the raging storm. Since the distance from Bangalore to the Gold Fields was not great, he could take his Enfield, leave me Muthuswamy and the Ambassador for my errands and meetings, and return home the same day for supper. He loved tooling around India on his motorcycle. Riding with him, I was always amazed at his ability to maneuver between bullock carts, beggars, and broken-down trucks loaded with livestock competing for space on India's dirt highways. He was so experienced and sure of himself on two wheels motorized, and the bloody chaos at such a far distance, that I did not worry about him. What happened next drove us away from even "safe" Bangalore.

Four months after Operation Blue Star on October 31, 1984, as Mrs. Gandhi walked the pathway from her walled residence in New Delhi to her office across the garden, she was met at the garden gate by two of her most trusted Sikh bodyguards. They turned their machine guns on her and continued the hail of bullets until she was dead. With the news of her death, Hindus immediately turned on the Sikh population wreaking vengeance throughout the streets of Delhi, its suburbs and other cities, killing whole families with rivers of petrol, setting fire to people, cars, homes, and shops while the police and army turned a blind eye. A few hours later when her son Rajiv was sworn in as Prime Minister, he beseeched his people to stop the "blood for blood." He ordered the military to restore order and set up refugee camps for the Sikh population as safe havens against the mobs. The rampage of Hindu hoodlums lasted three days and three nights nonetheless.

Since the seventies, this was the India that Yann Martel's now-famous character Pi and his family were hoping to escape from on the east coast in Pondicherry, where there was no certainty of peace, rule of law, or anything else enshrined in India's Constitution under Indira's dictatorial take-over of the country. This was the India that Mother Teresa and her flock of M.C. Sisters faced head-on with their mission to shelter and heal those who had no shelter against the rising tide of violence. This was the India that the British Raj had returned to its multitude of factions, all those princely states with their separate languages and customs trying reluctantly to fit under either the Muslim or Hindu umbrella and instead erupting almost daily in riots. This was the India that Cliff and I had decided to escape for a while in November 1984 with the promise of a respite in Darjeeling, certainly not with the expectation of finding and adopting a baby born on the doorstep of such conflagration.

Rajiv was new to politics. He had held office only four years since the untimely death of his brother Sanjay in 1980. Known on the campaign trail as "Mr. Clean," Rajiv's hands were unsullied, unlike his brother Sanjay's. The elder brother Rajiv, young, personable and with Bollywood good looks, had more interest in his career as an Indian Airlines pilot than he had in politics. But the tide of sympathy for his enormous loss was in his political favor. He decided to hold elections nonetheless.

Two weeks prior to the December 1984 elections, the worst industrial accident in human history struck central India's Bhopal. Very early on the morning of December 3, 1984 the white smoke from a gas-filled cloud began settling on the "City of Lakes" and one of India's greenest cities, no place for the deadly insecticide methyl isocyanate (MIC) or a chemical plant of any kind. Fits of coughing and vomiting and a burning sensation in the eyes roused people from their sleep. By dawn, the main streets were filled with people in search of safety. Some made it as far as the hospital. Many more did not.

You could say that American good will had ceased to be as

early as 1971 with Indira's signature on a twenty-year Treaty of Peace, Friendship, and Cooperation with the Soviet Union. Her decision was no doubt aided and abetted by Nixonian diplomacy that had sent a lethal flow of weapons into enemy West Pakistan in spite of mighty American congressional protest. But this was the last straw. The pesticide plant in Bhopal operated under joint agreement between Union Carbide and its local Indian affiliate, unlike most of the other multinationals that already had been nationalized. Although over 3,000 people were killed and hundreds of thousands were injured, the victims were paid little or nothing for fully seven years after the tragedy. And when Union Carbide finally settled, the Indian government kept the lion's share of the payment, doling out only US$ 550 to each of the victim's families.

1984, the year of our daughter's birth, or the daughter our hearts were set on, was a most turbulent year. Rajiv inherited from his mother her campaign promises made and not kept. He still had to face a nation of staggering poverty, over-population, political corruption, and food shortages, even though Indira had promised economic progress and social reform.

THE GENIE OF GRANT ROAD CROSS
A SHORT STORY

The morning Horatio Nelson Reid died, the crows were more eloquent than usual.

"Aw, Aw," they cried, black crabbed and hunched over the clothesline accusing. "What is there to recommend about people? That they slaughter one another in the streets? All we do is line fences together and flock to rooftops for no apparent reason. We are not shy and have many forms of laughter. Why then do these women veil their noses when we come only to peck at their feet?" Chorus ended, they flapped away.

It was hot and dry, coming on summer. The jacaranda spread flimsy blue canopies over Bangalore, and the moon shown through barred windows too bright for sleeping. Even in the cool of evening, the neighbor's children running around the yard chanting "Feedo, feedo" after their untethered puppy, rooms held the day's heat like skulls blistered and still feverish from the sun. Factory and ambulance sirens rose and faded into the distance. The brick-by-straw construction on the house next door at Grant Road Cross almost ceased.

It was the season of the cuckoo, or brain fever bird some call her. Never one to bother building her own nest, she had just moved into an abandoned crow's nest nearby. Even before dawn, she would attack the stillness with ever-widening loops, reaching higher and higher until she achieved a frenzied twirling that sounded out of mind. Someone in the neighborhood tried to dispel this new agitation with scratchy waltzes from an old record player. But she refused to be silenced. She managed to upstage even the most gregarious crows who kept low during these screaming cycles that raged on and on throughout the day. And when the rains came, they fell like buckets of stone on metal.

My neighbor Meena suggested we start our morning walks earlier. If we left for Cubbon Park before 7:00 a.m., right after the cow came to deliver the milk, we would avoid too much sun and the stench that rose from people's "misuse of the premises." Meena had a whole store of these euphemistic expressions, like "dustbins" for the stinking garbage heaps that drew cats, dogs, crows, enterprising servants, and certified rag-pickers in search of some little nourishment or discarded treasure. These sayings seemed quite natural, rolled pretty as the r's off her tongue. And being new to Bangalore, I was eager to understand as much of the local idiom as I could, like "acha" which I understood Meena to mean "okay." This she would follow with a graceful little head waggle I never quite managed to duplicate.

So with Mena in her carefully tucked saree and tennis sneakers, we passed dustbins and squatting figures on our way to the Park, saying pleasant, complimentary things about the morning. How brightly stood the cannas, we remarked to each other, and how the gulmohur tree was beginning to flame. Never mind the signs of "misuse" in the air.

On one of these morning strolls, when we had just escaped another hurtling bus by a tiger's eyetooth, Meena explained about "goondas."

"You have them over there," she said, "common thugs;

they're actually mere boys, paid to raise trouble." And then as an afterthought, "You mustn't call anyone that," and she laughed.

Goondas, so it seemed, were the malevolent tools of certain politicians making agitation in the City Market. Each morning the *Deccan Herald* brought word of another strike that turned violent and had to be subdued by police force. All of it inspired by some local film-star with political aspirations who wants to make the news, she summed it up. Meena had inside information of an official kind, since she used to play tennis with the chief of police, now retired.

"And you know, leaders are born of 'wiolence.'" Again the words rolled off her tongue like a lilting aphorism.

"Acha!" and we were off again headed for the Park.

The first time I laid eyes on Horatio Nelson Reid, he was standing hands on hips filling the corner gateway at Grant and Cross Roads like a small giant. Bald of head and belly, his massive frame was decorated in a red vest and short bloomer pants. Assorted bangles, ear loops, all conjured some fierce apparition uncorked from *One Thousand and One Nights*. He seemed to be surveying the road, a dusty thoroughfare coated with dog and ox dung, the crusty sediment from porridge vendors and paan stalls where men had left their betel nut chew on the ground for unsuspecting passers-by—not quite the kingdom a man of his stature would hope to command. And it showed in his furrowed, shiny brow. At the time, I thought he might be a more exotic form of California-grown tourist come to bask in the light of Sayd Baba or one of Bangalore's gurus, except for the way he possessed the land he stood on.

Again I saw him in the City Market, striding past fruit

and vegetable stalls, now and again stopping to inspect the tumbledown piles of papaya with great deliberation, as if he were mayor of the town dressed in marvelous disguise. He followed me into the sweet curds shop, bowed low with hands folded in a "Namaste" greeting, and tried to start a conversation standing way too close for my comfort zone.

"Too much of that stuff and you'll get fat," he said, which struck me as out of character for a proper genie, and I noticed he was wearing stained and dirty ankle supports. I mumbled something pleasant and headed out the door. If only I'd had the nerve, I would have presented my three wishes, or at least asked what the fancy get-up was all about.

Horatio had a sister, it was said, named Hattie Reid. For many years, Hattie ran Reid's Lodge, until her accumulation of dogs and a certain seedy reputation forced the place to close. Still there were a few lodgers, or fixed tenants. I knew this because near the first of each month she might stop me to beg money, only if Meena wasn't around.

"Do you have a rupee, dear?" she would ask in the most pitiful way, shaggy of clothes and hair, down to the last of her dog-filled days. "The rents are due, but I haven't even a rupee for a cigarette."

I would guess Hattie to be well into her fifties, but time and a penchant for excesses hadn't been kind. There was a certain boozy lackluster to her eyes; charcoal patches scarred her face. Aside from being stout and Anglo, she bore no resemblance whatsoever to Horatio. In contrast to his look of exuberant well-being and firm stance in the world, Hattie wore suspicion like a cruel eye-patch, never meeting your eyes unless, of course, there was the promise of a rupee. Cigarette dangling from a bitter mouth, she kept to herself and her one-woman mission feeding the street's skeletal dogs with paper cones full of rice. In a better life, she had been known as "Geraldine the Hairdresser," coifed and clad neat as a pin, it was said. But there were no signs of that life now.

According to Meena, they had terrible fights, Horatio and his sister. A year ago, after the death of their mother, he had come to Bangalore and moved into Hattie's lodge. He created quite a sensation because of his starring role in the film *Sinbad the Sailor*. Not that Bangalore was unaccustomed to celebrities. But these were mostly in the guru line, nothing so splendid as a foreign movie star, even an obscure one from an obscure porno film. He had hopes of landing some equally important role in the movie "A Passage to India," which was filming on location in Bangalore. But that did not work out, probably because he was too large for any of the leading parts. The role he auditioned for was given instead to Raj Fazal, the actor-turned-politician who was rumored to be the main force behind the strikes. Then David Lean's casting director failed to offer him so much as a spot in one of the crowd scenes.

Fascination over the genie on Grant Road dimmed as the "Passage" crew swept into town, and the fights between brother and sister escalated. She said that she would have thrown him out long ago, but she feared for her life. He said that the only thing she was afraid of was soap and water. At one point, when Horatio tried to assume the role of rent-collector at the lodge, the police had to be summoned to keep them from killing each other.

When the strikes began, they were sporadic at first. It was not unusual to be in Cubbon Park and see men gathered in clusters of half-dozen or more. Or you might see people clad all in white forming a long line that kept growing longer. A few stones were flung into windows; lorries carrying the daily news were overturned; some buses never finished their route. No one took these small incidents very seriously. They just preferred to avoid certain "troubled" districts.

Bangalore was known for keeping its famous garden city well tended and dispensing with undesirable elements, if need be. Hadn't the last uprising been efficiently squelched by a flourish of arms and freshly uniformed battalions? All these goondas required was a firm application of stick to knuckles. If the long uniform line suddenly broke and started running, you simply turned around and headed in the opposite direction—because Bangalore was a quiet town.

"Quark, Quark," said the crows, "a quiet town."

For a time I thought Horatio fancied me. He kept running into me literally over cucumbers and bananas and sweet curds, always with his same forceful physical presence and purposeful jabs at conversation. Later, when they resumed construction on the house next door, I discovered the real focus of his designs.

She arrived with the bricks—a tall, onyx statue shaped full in all the right places like a dancing Parvati. She stood out among the other construction workers, perhaps because of her bright pink saree and a movement that suggested a ship adrift. Each morning she came with a cart drawn by a pair of bullocks in matched purple horns and silver bells a-jangle. Gentle as the cart wheels' turning, she walked behind in cadence with the animals. On her hip, she carried a little girl, bare-bottomed but ribboned in pink to match the mother's saree. Against her easy stride, the child's chubby arms and legs bounced like parts of a rubber doll.

Once the child was deposited on a pile of bricks and left to play or fret, the woman filled her basket, lifted it to her head and then ever so gracefully passed out of sight into the stone cavity. After a time, she would emerge and begin again. Bend, lift. and carry. The motion became a rhythm until the light began to fade, the child was collected, and the cart moved clop-clop away.

Probably curious about this new activity in his domain, Horatio Nelson Reid came on his tour of inspection and stayed. At first he stationed himself unobtrusively behind a wall and then found an open gate that would support his weight and give a better view. As time went on and the bullocks chewed their fill of the neighborhood vines, the cart began to leave without the pink-clad form. More and more, she became a presence, tucking stray hair into her braid, or bending down to rub a bruise on the child's leg.

I don't remember ever seeing Horatio and the woman speak directly to one another, perhaps because Horatio did not speak Tamil. But he did carry on with the child and she chattered back at him, while the mother looked on. Between those dark arms folded over the wall, her smile was like a slice of the moon she shone on Horatio and the guards and the vendors cycling by. I sometimes wondered if Horatio noticed. Whatever communication he managed to develop with the mother seemed to pass through the child. And it grew friendlier as the child became less a creature of brick dust and more a little girl in bright new ribbons and store-bought dresses.

He used to come around quitting time in full genie regalia with some small package, and you would see the three of them in a huddle. The child held the center of the circle, the mother's low notes weaving a warm music around the high-pitched laughter, and the genie beaming over all.

Once he brought an old copper pot and with a lot of gesturing managed to persuade the child to rub it. She rubbed and rubbed with her tiny fist, Horatio lifted the attached lid, and out fluttered a bright green parakeet—a little dazed but airborne. The child screamed with delight. Thereafter the pot was her constant companion. She would sit on the edge of Grant Road, cradling it in her arms and rubbing furiously. Then she would lift the lid and peer inside. Over and over, she seemed content to replay Horatio's original stunt, no matter the results.

Horatio was accomplished at all sorts of magic, the now-you-see-it-now-you don't kind. He could materialize silk scarves, paper flowers, shiny one-rupee coins. And the child was his best audience. In another setting they might have made something of a circus act—the giant sprung from Aladdin's lamp and his live brown Kewpie-doll.

On Sundays Horatio would come to fetch them with a lunch basket. The woman's hair was always shiny then, washed of its pink dust, oiled and plaited with strong-scented garlands of jasmine flowers. Off they would go for an outing in Cubbon Park at a slow, leisurely pace so that the child could keep up. She bounced along on her thick round legs, one hand holding tight to Horatio's, the other fastened to the copper pot clattering down the street. The woman followed several respectful paces behind.

After some weeks, the absent father, sober and repentant, showed up to reclaim his family. There wasn't any confrontation, perhaps because the man was so small Horatio could have snuffed him out with a firm squeeze. I suspect Horatio didn't want any more trouble with the police, what with their growing hostility over the strikes. Anyway, he sort of faded back into Hattie's domain with the dogs—perhaps biding his time until the competition went on another binge.

I remember one night coming home late. We turned into Grant Cross and the headlights shone on a figure standing firm in the middle of the road with legs spread apart. There was no mistaking him. It was Horatio armed with a thick red stick as if poised for some attack. No, the power in that stance suggested a man looking for trouble. Something about that dark encounter, the way he stepped out of the shadows, made me shutter. We didn't waste any time getting inside the house.

As I was saying, Bangalore was a quiet town, some might even say sleepy, and safe enough for the wealthy of India to build so many retirement homes. People righteously criticized too much industrial development. It was spoiling the town's congenial weather. Despite the fuss, most people privately supported these signs of progress. And no one took the strikes very seriously, believing in Bangalore's essential peace and prosperity. Besides the trouble was safely far from the old British civil lines that still marked the polite side of town. It was confined to the more congested districts known to harbor goondas and other querulous elements, places where the bodies of men and dogs put down to sleep or die, places like Russell Market, Tannery, and Old Poor House Roads, the Bamboo Bazaar.

I don't know why they called the Bazaar that, because I never saw anything like bamboo there, only a hazy winding lane of stalls stacked with gray jungle-wood shaped for use in construction, each stall a dark replica of the next. It smelled of dust and dry wood and tinder about to catch, which happened frequently during the Divali celebrations. A few over-zealous revelers lighting fire-crackers reduced the Bazaar to a smoldering heap of charcoal and rubble, and then they would somehow reconstruct it all over again—year after year.

This wasn't the Divali season, but things were going up in smoke anyway. Somebody arrested for stealing a bicycle had just died in the Shivajinagar jail and the mob outside the jail turned nasty. The police commissioner was struck full in the back with a huge stone, and his force had to turn back men bent on setting fire to the station. Even so, rebuke was mild. A few rounds were fired in the air, some teargas clouded the by-lanes, and a curfew kept the area quiet at least from dusk to dawn.

Next day the police fought off the stones with more teargas, rubber bullets, and lathi-charges with long, metal-tipped wooden sticks. That was after the dead man's father, one Munna Gafar, ageing and retired after selling off his meat stall, it was reported, found his son's body at the mortuary bearing several marks of injury and torture. The crowd demanded simple justice—suspension of the police officers responsible for the death, a proper burial with all the rites, jobs for the jobless who would be led into a life of stealing bicycles. In answer to these simple demands, the police gave them live bullets.

At this point, Raj Fazal, Bangalore's leading film star, got into the act. Since the Gafar family was part of his constituency, he felt compelled to go and help them claim the dead son's body, so he said. Then again on "humanitarian grounds" he went to the police station to pacify the crowds gathered there. Instead the mob turned even more unruly and Fazal was arrested for instigating a riot. This launched his fans on a rampage of burning and looting. All of it made the news, especially the Mahatma Gandhi-inspired loincloth of coarse home-spun cotton khadi and shawl which Fazal wore to the hasty funeral.

What took Horatio Nelson Reid into the troubled Shivajinagar market is anybody's guess. Maybe he wanted a piece of the action or maybe he went to buy more pink ribbons. Perhaps he only wanted to see the pyrotechnics. He wore the look of having just materialized from a column of smoke.

The police were storming a certain house on Old Poor House Road known to be manufacturing petrol bombs. Small fires set here and there along the road made it virtually impassable, like the rim of a flaming inferno. Smoke belched out of the Gandhi Bhavan Hotel. A few cars and auto-rickshaws were ablaze. Men with torches ran against the tide of police. When they stumbled or were trampled in the muck of overturned fruit carts, they were showered with blows and beaten to their knees. Some darted toward the safety of the doors of the suspicious house but found them bolted. Faces peered out of darkened rooms, gaunt, unblinking. Trails of charcoal scarred the hot ball of sun going down.

Whether he volunteered or the job was thrust of upon him, Horatio took on a supervisory role in the melee that followed the police charge on the house. All of a sudden, he was seen beating out the flaming dustbins with his red vest, raising pushcarts, fallen signs, and bodies, as if to recompose the narrow street's geography. Empowered by some obscure force, his massive chest and arms worked like a shiny steel earth-mover, lifting immovable objects and depositing them out of harm's way. Caught between walls of flame, his body glistened through the smoke and teargas. Scrawny-legged men in dusty white dhotis scrambled out of his path. Bullocks and horses stampeded, wild-eyed in their frenzy to escape. He seemed to be issuing orders, and a few brave souls stopped to listen.

"I am here, Master. I am here," he kept shouting above the infernal din. No one could make any instruction out of that. So the human engine continued alone, repairing the world by a simple command and a rub from some heaven-bound source. Body straining under the weight of this new calling, Horatio raised more smoke and dust and debris and flailing bodies, muttering, "I am here," to which the crows answered from a very safe distance, "Now. Now."

Horatio was raised up like a pillar supporting a slab of stone when a round of gunfire cracked the air. Like a slow-motion fade-out, the giant frame crumbled as it took the ammunition, live bullets or not, no one could say for sure in the dense cloud that filled the road. And finally, there he was, a heap of flesh and jewels lying face-down in the dung, his ankles still wearing their soiled bandages. A police wagon arrived to cart him away, and when the hour of his abandoned life came no one knew exactly.

That's when the rains started, gentle at first. Then they came down pelting hard, like an over-generous offering of peace. My neighbor Meena's promise of "April showers" struck with enough ferocity to tear immense limbs from Cubbon Park's grandest and toughest old trees.

Hattie abandoned her dogs for a day to go through the rivers of mud to claim the body. The woman in pink moved herself and her child into the shelter of the skeletal construction.

She tried making conversation with our night watchman. When the lorry came to take the scaffolding away, she and the child went with it.

Chapter 9

WHERE TO GET HELP

T oward the end of November 1984, about three weeks after
*that fateful trip to Darjeeling followed by the devastating meeting
with Sister Margaret Mary at the Motherhouse in Calcutta, we
are having no luck in our attempts to reach Mother Teresa in
person. We are desperate for help of any kind. Jane says she will
ask her photojournalist friend Raghu Rai to use his influence.
He and Mother have developed a very favorable relationship
over many years of photo sessions with her. Also Jane suggests I
represent the* Straits Times *and use the newspaper as an excuse
to meet with Mother. Once we are in her presence, we can press
the question of adoption. But to my every attempt, the response
from the Missionaries of Charity is that Mother is either out-of-
station, or too busy, or too ill.*

~

To reach Mother, I reasoned, we would have to use what-
ever influential contacts we had developed so far in India.
Since I could think of no one and had heard nothing from
Raghu Rai, Jane suggested I write to Minu, the wife of the
U. N. High Commissioner for Refugees in Singapore, Shashi
Tharoor. We knew them only casually through friends at the

American Embassy there. I do recall turning up at the same dinner party once. They were Indian and influential, and Minu had just given birth to twins, said Jane. I write her a very carefully worded letter.

> *17 Grant Road Cross*
> *Bangalore 560 001*
> *India*
> *29 November 1984*

Dear Minu,

Jane has urged me to write you in the event that you or your family can help us. Here's the story: Cliff and I have fallen in love with a baby girl in Darjeeling. A few hours after her delivery on 10 November at Victoria Hospital, she somehow came to the Missionaries of Charity with no name, perhaps the child of a college student from Sikkim.

I report to you what we were told by the supervising nun there, Sister Jean. She sent us down the mountain to the Children's Home in Tindharia for "paperwork" and consultation with Sister Dionysia supposedly to start adoption procedures; however, in Tindharia we learn from Sister Dionysia that all the children of that region who come to the Missionaries of Charity are to be adopted locally or go to homes in Belgium, Italy, or France— anyway not to Americans. But we should go ahead and appeal to Sister Margaret Mary at the M.C. in Calcutta.

In Calcutta we meet with Sister Margaret Mary to no avail. To every plea, no and no and no. Reason being, as best I could understand, that all the various adoption agencies have sort of parceled out the subcontinent amongst themselves so that they keep everything orderly and don't infringe on each other's territory. These babies go here, and those babies go there. I can understand the need to regulate adoption procedures in India, but saying that we can't have her because her location is wrong simply makes no sense to me.

As the rules have been established between these agencies, we can never have a mountain child. They are not in our "zone." And it is the mountain child we are most attracted to, namely this mountain child. Sister Margaret Mary tried to make us believe that these tribal children aren't very bright, tend to be sickly, commonly TB and eardrum infections from the severe cold, and all the while I am thinking how I just want to go back up there and gather her up now and bring her to this more hospitable climate in Bangalore. It's so cold there, even in Tindharia, her next destination. I want to give her every possible chance, make sure she gets whatever medical attention she needs before it's too late (she had a nasty case of diarrhea) and the mother's love she needs now. Not two years from now. Two years is the normal length of time foreign adoptive parents must wait for a baby born in India. Minu, the children in these homes looked so listless, so pinched with worry around the eyes, or maybe I was projecting my own anxieties on them—but I don't think so. Surely the earlier a baby finds her own home the better. Yes?

I can't say Sr. MM was insensitive to our hearts, just quite firm. The International Mission of Hope has nice babies, too, she told us, and they're the ones destined for the States, also non-sectarian. But the woman in charge won't be back from the U. S. until January. I am dizzy looking at so many babies (it's taking on the air of a sale at Macy's) and none of them beautiful as this baby. But at least at the International Mission of Hope we were told of the need for a "home study," step number one in the sequence toward guardianship, and this we have arranged.

What we must know is this: Is Sister Margaret Mary the last

*word on our baby, or is there some higher authority to whom we
can appeal? Should we petition Mother Teresa directly, or can
someone more influential do that on our behalf? Might the baby
be transferred to an American-approved agency, or is she bound
to the M. C. (and the Catholic Church)? Neither of us is Catholic
(well, Cliff was so christened but that's the extent of his association). Is there some way we might skirt the agency rules and
arrange guardianship—the sooner the better? I can go anywhere
in a moment's notice. Oh yes, forgot, we would have tried to see
Mother Teresa herself if she had been in station.*

*Points in our favor: we expect to be residing in India indef-
initely as our company contract is open-ended and Bangalore
suits us quite nicely. Therefore we'll be in no rush to make her an
American citizen, if that is a consideration. And mainly, we can
give her a loving family and quite comfortable home immediately.
We have no phone as yet (although we have been on the waiting
list for almost a year) but can be reached through our neighbor
Kavery in Bangalore at 568764 and here is Cliff's card attached.*

*If there is a way you can help lead us out of this labyrinth, we'll
be ever so grateful. And the warmest congratulations to you and
Shashi on your own pair of joys,*
Bonnie
*P.S. I just read this over and it seems so rushed, Minu. I just
hope you can make sense of it and hear my heart.*

On 10 December, Minu's husband Shashi sent a kind and
sympathetic reply on behalf of both of them from Bombay,
saying that Minu had her hands full with the twins.

Dear Bonnie –
Your moving letter of November 28 has just arrived. Minu is

too overwhelmed by the twins these days that our correspondence is now, more than ever, my responsibility! I hope you do not mind hearing from me this time around, on both our behalfs.

We have thought about your problem and made some enquiries. My mother (with whom we are camping now) volunteered for years at Shishu Bhavan in Calcutta while my parents were posted there and has some idea too of the way things work. The general consensus is that the bureaucratization of the adoption process is a fact of life from which it is not going to be easy to escape through conventional means. The best—indeed perhaps the only—thing to do in this situation would be to appeal to Mother Teresa personally. This will mean trying to track her down—a letter may be handled by one of her staff and never get to her. If you find access very difficult (which shouldn't be the case, but these days you never know) you must mention that you wish to interview her for the Straits Times and discuss a personal matter with her.

"I hope things will work out. Minu will, in the meantime, take the matter up with some journalist friends here who know the Calcutta situation, and see if she can unearth any better ideas. If any of us have anything better to suggest, you'll hear from us.

"Good luck and all the best in the New Year—Shashi"

~

At home in Bangalore, I was doing battle with deities other than the Catholic Church. The flower thief, a regular early morning visitor, came to strip my gangly bougainvillea of its frail blossoms for some distant temple god. I told our watchman Balraj to somehow communicate to this woman with her pincers on the end of a bamboo pole that this, too, was a temple and that she was stealing flowers from temple gods.

"Yes, memsahib," Balraj would bob his head dutifully and straighten his back with the purpose his wrinkled khaki

Sister Dionysia

uniform promised. "I will take up the matter with her." But the sneaky lady came too early in the morning for anyone to catch her. Perhaps we were harboring the wrong "gods."

In spite of Sr. Margaret Mary's unhappiness with our lack of Catholic faith, we were not devoid of religion. We had been full-time attenders at the Quaker Meeting in Singapore, also known as the Religious Society of Friends. And Cliff was leaning on the side of Buddhism, ever since Vietnam and his experience of a hilltop temple south of Bien Hoa. It was near a major airbase off noisy Highway One and provided the quiet he desperately needed. Now he was studying the literature and going in search of other Buddhist temples for the peace he felt there. The teachings and meditative practice seemed to be helping his demons. Of course we were not about to share that information with Sr. Margaret Mary.

With a few other long-time Quakers, I was actively trying to re-establish the Meeting for Worship in Bangalore. P. T.

Thomas was doing all the leg-and-paper work, and Cliff and I were providing a meeting place in our home on Grant Road Cross. We few Quaker stalwarts gathered for worship on each First Day (Sunday) in the traditional silent manner, according to the teachings of the founder of the faith, George Fox. The tiny flock, composed about half and half of Indian and British in addition to us, sat comfortably in our living room, some with heads bowed and eyes closed, others looking straight ahead, all waiting for a message to share inspired by the companionship, the silence, and God's presence. The un-programmed Meeting for Worship held to the idea that Quakers, or Friends, could find spiritual truth through inward searching and group discernment.

The hour passed quickly or slowly, depending on each one's meditative state. We broke the silence by standing and holding hands around the circle and then moved to the dining table, where I had laid out the makings of tea. And in the Quaker tradition, we discussed matters of peaceful activism, where we could be most useful, such as in writing letters to the *Deccan Herald*, visiting politicians, boycotting offensive establishments and services. Especially in the aftermath of the upheaval in the Punjab and the disaster in Bhopal, the possibilities for activism were endless.

Marjorie Sykes, that doyenne of the Quaker movement in India, was "holding us in the Light," both our quest for the baby and the establishment of the Worship Group. She sent regular letters of encouragement and visited us from her Friends Rural Centre at Rasulia, Hoshangabad in Madhya Pradesh. Rasulia was one of the beacons of light in the movement toward natural farming and away from India's attempts to achieve larger agricultural surpluses with fertilizers and pesticides, like the ones produced at Bhopal only an hour's ride away. During that disaster, the town of Hoshangabad welcomed the thousands fleeing from Bhopal, and the Quakers did what they could to help.

In *The Friendly Way*, the little Quaker magazine Marjorie and P. T. Thomas edited for the Asia-Pacific region, she wrote in February 1985:

> *"The disaster has not left many destitute orphans. Sadly, little children were more vulnerable than their parents; there were heavy child casualties. Many orphans are with relatives; the Government has housed others at the School for the Blind and Deaf–Mute (with which we were favorably impressed) and is trying to trace their kinfolk....*
>
> *"In conclusion, there is very little that can be done in Bhopal by outside agencies or outside money. But there is a great deal that can be done, in India and outside India, to raise public awareness of the factors which led to the disaster—aside from the more obvious ones. There should be an urgent re-appraisal of the need for poisonous pesticides in agriculture. Rasulia and other agencies are working hard to demonstrate viable alternatives. Bhopal was a traumatic shock, but almost every week, for many years, some obscure corner of some newspaper has carried a paragraph about the poisoning of field workers using pesticide sprays, or through accidental contamination of food. These casualties are reported— and forgotten. But their total could far exceed Bhopal."*

My thought was if only more attention had been paid to Marjorie and her team of farmers when Indira purchased whole-sale the "green revolution" at such great cost to her land and her people.

In her own quiet way, Marjorie was doing the work of Mother Teresa, but in places where the need was different. Like Mother, Marjorie had come to India at about the same time as a young girl to teach girls.

This freedom-fighter friend of Gandhi worked as a teacher in his ashram for 10 years. Under the influence of Gandhi and the poet Tagore, she had stayed on in India to work for peace and compulsory education for all. In the 1960s she took on the work of the Nagaland Peace Mission, which was mainly concerned with implementing the terms of the ceasefire agreement between the Naga rebels and the Indian government. With her colleagues in the Mission, for three years Marjorie worked to remove friction through personal contacts—in the Quaker tradition of spreading peace in the world.

The incomparable 80-year-old wore her white hair as straight and no-nonsense as her calling to follow Gandhi's path. She found herself quite at home at my desk and manual typewriter. In her antique briefcase she carried a soon-to-be-published manuscript full of delightfully told "Gandiji" memories. She wore the coarse cotton khadi someone long ago had spun on Gandhi's loom and was most distressed about our plumbing—the terrible waste of cold water before you got to the hot. She taught me the fine art of ragi porridge with jaggery (the black bits of coal do settle on the bottom of the boil) and she left her wonderful presence and her socks in our home for many days.

~

The Quaker Meeting we attended in Singapore had been an essential part of our life there. In addition to finding great spiritual sustenance in the gatherings and teachings, I counted that group the hub of my social life—an international circle of activist writers, teachers, and doctors. We kept up a lively correspondence from India and when we returned on leave to Singapore that Christmas 1984, it was a return to the warm, welcoming arms of the Friends.

Also in Quaker circles the Singapore Meeting was renowned for some of its principle members. It was Tom Silcock, a Quaker expat teaching at Raffles College in Singapore, who came up with the idea of a union to protect Singapore's taxi drivers and was instrumental in forming the now famous NTUC, National Trades Union Congress. Professor Eric Holttum, the Director of Singapore Botanic Gardens from 1926 to1949, had been a major public figure during his tenure both at the Gardens and at the University of Malaya. I counted his important contribution to the Gardens especially during the Japanese occupation as part of my inspiration for taking on the book project and valued his warm correspondence until his death in 1990.

Two sisters, Dr. Lau Wai Har, head of Singapore's ministry of education, and Dr. Lau Wai Ping, retired TB specialist, hosted the Meeting at their penthouse flat in one of the original high-rise buildings behind the Istana, the President's official residence. Collectors of Chinese antiquities, they filled their walls with scrolls of brush-painted birds and fish and cabinets displaying jade carvings, green celadon, and blue and white porcelain bowls.

We sat on heavily carved teak chairs polished to a dark glow around a thick woolen carpet patterned with camels shaped like Tang dynasty tomb figures. I remember the camels well for having stared into them with head bowed during so many hours of worship. Ours was the traditional hour-long silent worship interrupted only when a member of the group felt compelled to share a message. It amazed me how often the messages spoken even by strangers during Quaker Meeting seemed meant for my ears.

As I sat in that gathered meeting at Christmas 1984, "gathered" in the Quaker sense of all the members being united in the silence, someone's mention of Jonathan Livingston Seagull brought to mind another Richard Bach reference, one from *Illusions*: "In every problem to overcome, there is a gift." If I could write a book, I ruminated, meet the challenges of demanding jobs, live like the cuckoo in borrowed nests all over the world, come to the blank page every day with only a passing hope of some spark of creativity or truth to this single-minded experience, if I could depend on the generosity of God to fill my days with love and friendship and work, this heart's work, if I could keep listening at this small outpost of faith—well, I could care for someone else's child as if she were my own for a very long time. Something about that baby, vulnerable, homeless, and utterly dependent, beautiful and new, perfect in the shape of her tiny fingers and ears, a gift of creation, settled me firmly on that carpet.

Chapter 10

INDIA FEVER

At this stage in the venture, the New Year 1985, while I am falling in love with India, Cliff is preparing to leave India. Already he is doing the mapping and mental work for a new assignment in China. There is no way I can leave this place. Not now. I refuse to leave without possession of that baby, by some miracle or the other.

~

On that return to Singapore for the Christmas holiday, timed for Cliff to meet with the regional company executives to discuss China, we learned that the western world had gone India crazy. Its origin was largely in the popular entertainment media, and more specifically the spate of Raj nostalgia films coming out of the UK. There was the popular *Jewel in the Crown* mini-series on TV based on Paul Scott's *Raj Quartet*, David Attenborough's film *Gandhi* that swept the Oscars just in 1982, and now David Lean's new film *A Passage to India*. Add to that the handsome face of Indira's son Rajiv Gandhi and perhaps some conscience raised over Bhopal.

The Raj mystique must still have been stored in India's

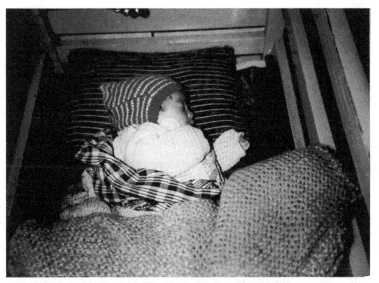

Pema at Tindharia M.C. orphanage

attics, although most of that generation had grown beyond the septuagenarian by now. Apart from what looked like Camelot in New Delhi with Rajiv and his beautiful Italian bride Sonia, such a vast improvement over Indira, there was hope in the wind again as there was during Independence, they said. At least his mother was gone, as well as her finger ever pointing at the "foreign influence" (aka American) behind all of India's ills. Like an antidote to disaster, Rajiv Gandhi had emerged with a strong sense of leadership and handsome youthfulness bringing a feeling of renewed vigor and great expectations for the future of India in the world.

Still, in most of the India I visited, I observed places like Bhopal, a town of green hills and streams once unspoiled where humble folk were proud to live. Now they were teetering on the brink of disaster with twentieth-century technology which they were simply not prepared for or really cared for. All that sophisticated equipment did not bring the education or the West's drive to get and spend on the corporate level.

Some of Cliff's colleagues in the states were sending him resumes and querying him about employment "in some exciting location like Bangalore or other exotic locations in India." Cliff suggested they see *Passage* to get an idea of life here, since it had been filmed just last year in Bangalore and nothing had changed here since the British left.

Actually the *Passage* film sets made vast improvements over last February's dust-covered Bangalore. Mind you, it hadn't rained here since December. The film crew had virtually moved into Bangalore during the month of March 1984. For the sake of crowd control, they recreated most of the town of Chandrapore on the site of the old abandoned Maharaja's Palace. Built in the early days of the Raj to resemble Balmoral, the Queen's estate in Scotland, the Palace stretched to three times the size of the original. The made-for-movie, mile-long market glowed with brightly colored squashes that looked to be hand-painted. No sign of fly-infested beast or fowl carcass hung from the bazaar rafters. The Bangalore Club, once the hub of Raj social life, looked permanently starched white for tea-time. To be sure, no wall surface displayed cow-pies, those ubiquitous cakes of dung shaped with cut straw into precious cooking fuel for the peasants and plastered on walls all across Bangalore. In India, no one tried to hide the omnipresent poverty, except in David Lean's film.

Since the color of the true railroad station didn't suit the Director, he stopped production for two days while they repainted the entire station. Then they added a bright red strip at the bottom of the engine to give just the right effect when the train pulled into the station. Irritation grew into outrage uniting the town as soon as the film crew took the liberty of blasting and drilling into the rock face at Savandurga to create the fictional Marabar Caves. The chosen site, a huge mountain landscape at the Savandurga village in Magadi taluk, handily just 30 km west of Bangalore, had no caves. The real Barabar Caves that Forester had described in the novel were not considered grand enough for an epic film. Besides, these caves were located in the impoverished state of Bihar, up in the far north-east corner of the subcontinent just under Nepal, far away from picturesque Bangalore.

In David Lean's favor, however, he did make an acceptable contribution to the temple located on top of Savandurga and managed to seal most of the holes when filming finished. In the end, they drilled only six to eight feet into the rock in a few places and then recreated the rest of the cave interior back home in their studios in England.

Of course, the film had yet to reach India, some 10 months after the launch. David Lean wouldn't want to waste his premiers on any third-world audience, even if they were the subject and substance of his film about Anglo-Indian relations in British-colonized India. Everyone in Bangalore, therefore, from the lowliest vendors to the sahibs and memsahibs, was anxious to see their faces or familiar places.

With my newfound journalistic skills, I did try to interview David Lean but had the same luck as with Mother Teresa. This time it was the wife who stood in the way. She was full of excuses. The film-making wonder aged 75 was too busy, too tired, too behind schedule. They were hoping to wrap up the Bangalore filming soon and needed no more delays before the move to Kashmir to finish with the India-based part of the filming. I had even taken the time to re-read *Passage* and was full of questions about which scenes he had chosen to film and why. The sting of insult lifted when I met his art director later at a social gathering. With no little bitterness, he dismissed the famous film director.

"Throughout the filming, Lean didn't even so much as bid me a good morning."

~

So much of our first year had been taken up with the difficulties of adjusting to life in India, although they paled in the light of India's troubled history that year. Bangalore was a sociable place, even more so than Singapore. People would drop in regularly unannounced and stay and stay, and talk your ear off. I guess it was one of the few forms of entertainment, aside from a Rotary Club event. That uniquely American institution was very big here. There were a variety of evening cocktail/late supper circuits we might have joined, were we so inclined, but all this sociability lent itself to a manana attitude that rivaled the Mexican. Because Cliff had to WORK under these conditions and had some very demanding requirements states-side where they are used to double-time efficiency (not to mention his own extreme work ethic), it was a struggle for him to keep up with any sort of social life.

The first two weeks of January he spent at Singrauli, south of Delhi at one of Coal India's infamous guest houses, where he would be lucky to find even a dirty sheet on the cot or a learner-cook. Workers had no access to even the simplest tools for minimal truck maintenance and everybody else was an "Engineer" who wouldn't dare soil his hands with some real experience. With so much safety-training and safety-consciousness, Cliff was a real case by the time he returned home. The guest-house diet of rice and ghee sent his triglycerides into orbit—and so I worried about all these hazards, even knowing that underneath he welcomed the adventure and the stories he could tell. But the job was tough on the system in other ways. Cliff was the one who had to say yes or no to the claims for financial loss the Indian collaborator (B.E.M.L., Bharat Earth Movers Limited) sought, not a popular job, like a fall guy who's caught in the bad feelings between India and the U.S. Sometimes, to him, the dilemma did seem overwhelming. But he had made some good friends and trained some good people. He did not find the fishing he had hoped for, except for some yet unexplored possibilities. He could escape now and then on his Enfield (classic made-in-India motorcycle)—shades of Darth Vader in helmet and black leather jacket. For more fun, he built some shelves into his office where he tinkered with electronic devices and made a transistor radio of most distinct sound clarity.

Of course, nothing ever worked right here. Three bathrooms were a plumbing disaster. I usually had to help guests with the flush. After about a year in our newly constructed bungalow, cracks were forming in the sinks and puddles from unknown sources seeping onto the floor. Do I mention this when Cliff arrives home Saturday night, or maybe wait a few days for a more fortuitous moment, before the ship sinks? All these fancy repairs call for "Super Wrench," who more than once has employed such abusive language that I expect our neighbors to send their violin-toting children off to convent school.

I was glad for a rejuvenation of Friends Quaker Meeting here. The most intriguing and mysterious of all the visitors

to our Meeting was the tiny wisp of a brown man, dear
Radjasekharan, the image of M. Gandhi himself in his last
years down to his stubbly white head and grasshopper knees.
His traditional khadi shirt and pajamas were immaculately
white and crisp. On entering my front door, he removed
a pair of dusty black dress shoes—a rarity in sandal-clad
India—easily two sizes too large and with such grace that
no one seemed to notice.

Whether it was due to his accent or the soft gumming of
his words, we caught only pieces of his story. He had worked
at the U. N., he said, and lived for a while in New York and
Geneva. To all our questions, he gave the same reply. Yes, he
had worked at the U. N.

He moved freely about the downstairs of our house
inspecting things, trying every drawer and lid and then he
would stand back, hands on hips, in a sort of amused satisfaction. Some lively conversation must have been going on
inside his head. Eventually he did find a chair, settled in the
lotus position and began to meditate. The rest of us followed
suit, in the "gathering" tradition of Quakers. He spoke of St.
Paul in a diction marked with oratory, some verses he had
read recently about conquering the passions. If we were to
have peace among nations, he posited, we would first have
to make peace within ourselves, a most arduous task because
of all these passions, sex and anger and jealousy that keep
acting up.

After he had taken tea, he wandered all over my downstairs in search of the newspaper which he read in a corner
to himself. When he rejoined us, he apologized for spilling a
few drops of tea on the floor and chuckled to himself. Then
he waded into the boats of his oversized black shoes and was

gone. No amount of protest would keep him longer and no, he needed no assistance finding his way. We puzzled over what seemed a strange, almost mythic apparition. Was he a reincarnation of Gandiji or just deaf as a stone? Sadly, we haven't seen him since.

~

For myself, after more than a year in Bangalore, I find India surprisingly hospitable just as I must be coming to appreciate some dark side of my soul. It is a life-changing place I feel I have been wandering toward for a very long time. The experience of home-leave says a lot. Once we are returned "safely" to the States' familiarity where everything runs smoothly, we find little to keep us there. Here, there is some satisfaction in knowing that we support five families, those of our so-called "servants" and that our presence is needed in so many other less obvious ways. I do a little volunteer work each week, when I am not absorbed in the piles of paperwork to get Pema. I've gotten over the impulse to tidy up all of India and bring every hungry-looking child home. And I know that I shall never know all I want to about this immense land so full of contrarities, but the challenge keeps me questing. Perhaps I have been cast under the same spell as Adela Quested in the first chapter of *Passage*. I am determined to see the "real" India before quitting her.

Morning comes early, the call to prayer from the nearby mosque at about 5:30 a.m., and I have to see what the *mali* is up to. Early on we put in a garden. Now tall cannas, hibiscus, miniature roses and nameless pots line the drive, bougain-villea spills over the walls in assorted colors, and the stubby grass mostly keeps the good earth from seeping inside the house. There's a young sandalwood and an old champaka that stretches its branches onto our bedroom balcony. Sometimes our ayah Kamala slips the fragrant blossoms under our pillows.

I love the clear light here. It fills my study all day with friendliness and provides the right acoustics to practice my flute. I don't feel caught between high-rise towers or am I gasping for breath and energy as I did in Singapore's humidity. If the streets are messy, at least they show their affinity with Mother Earth. Everything grows in untamed abundance, with here and there a re-shaping of Nature's extravagance.

The pleasures are so simple—the cacophony of street noises and birdsong, a few good friends, and regular haunts—markets, bookstalls, parks, crumbling streets, and crumbling old mansions. I turn every corner and still find infinite wonder, suspect I will even if I live here the rest of my life, which may be required if ever I hope to have Pema. I see it all gradually becoming a part of my vocabulary, and I've learned to wheel and deal with the best of the street-vending *wallas* (now that may be some exaggeration). And this room of my own to which I come in sickness and in health to write and play my flute is a clean well-lighted place, never mind the gnat covered clutters. They are somehow purposeful.

I only wish Cliff could find it a more comfortable place. I can't fully appreciate the rigor of his work. I don't experience the same level of incompetence and discomfort and arrogance that he does when he's on the road and in the office. But I know that he's found little to keep him here and that makes me wonder about our future, the next move, and I don't want to leave India—not now when I have found a home and perhaps a family.

~

While Cliff was in Singrauli, we had a strange visitation. A young silver-grey owl perched just here on the doorstep to my study balcony. The crows were raising a ruckus, and I feared for its small life. Now I have heard plenty of owls in and out of my sleep but never actually seen one. I remember once late at night stepping onto our patio in Indianapolis, alone and deeply troubled. I let go with the words of some poem-in-the-making, and this owl sort of answered back. So here before my eyes was this remarkable creature, so still and uncertain about its future with eyes as dark and far-reaching as India's ancient forests. I wish I could describe the mysterious depth in those eyes.

Our favorite watchman Balraj told me to say not a word. Among some Hindus, he warned, the presence of an owl spells disaster.

"They call for the priest and pujah with cow urine and holy water from the Ganges, Memsahib. They will shut down your house for weeks to dispel the evil spirits." And all I feel here are good spirits. Sadly, the owl took off, flying utterly silent toward the neighbor's house. The crows were quick to follow. A gray feather floating on the air was the last I saw of it.

Chapter 11
MOUNTAINS OF PAPERWORK

It is March 1985. We are growing impatient and losing hope. After visits to Calcutta and numerous other places, it seems likely that we cannot have Pema, the adoption process in India being the morass of red tape that it is. Still I am not giving up. I loved her when I saw her, but with all the waiting, I am beginning to worry that time is running out on me here at mid-life. I wonder how a pregnant mother must feel. Surely it cannot be any more difficult for her or emotionally painful. And she has the advantage of carrying the baby with her.

~

From November 1984 onward, Cliff stayed on the road or in the air pretty constantly visiting mining sites, while I tried to keep up with the adoption paperwork at home. When meetings called him to Calcutta, he could work in a quick trip north to Tindharia to see the baby and bring back pictures.

For the first time, I could see her eyes wide open, dark, and almond-shaped. The photographs Cliff took showed her in a pointy elfin cap, striped red and white, and an oversized sweater with a dog and other cartoon figures under the word "Wednesday" printed in faded pastel colors. She was under a heavy crocheted blanket, her little arms raised with tiny fists poking the air. A circle of tin bells hung above her head out of reach. The whole assorted and mismatched scene spoke to me of hand-made charitable gifts that had been donated to keep the babies warm.

On his first trip to visit the baby in the Tindharia orphanage, Cliff was in a taxi driving from Siliguria when he saw on the side of the road nuns wearing the white and blue striped sarees characteristic of Mother's Missionaries of Charity. He told the driver to pull over to see if he could help. There she was, Sister Dionysia, looking as if she were expecting him.

"This is no surprise. I knew you would come," she said. But Cliff was surprised that she should recognize him at all having seen him only once nearly three months ago. She had just purchased a load of wood for the orphanage, at a very good price, she said. But her old Ambassador could not carry her six passengers plus the wood. Cliff helped load the wood in his taxi and took on two passengers, one of them Sr. Dionysia's brother.

At the orphanage, she handed Cliff our baby pointing out the dark birthmarks to prove she was "the original." Soon Pema fell asleep in Cliff's arms but not before wetting the knee of his pants.

"Oh, your daughter has given you a gift," and the Sister laughed.

In answer to Cliff's consternation about the hold-up in our adoption, Dionysia explained the history behind the current system of Indian adoptions. Some years ago Marxist agitators had tried to block all foreign adoptions by spreading the rumor that Indian children were being raised as slaves in foreign countries. For a time, the rumors they spread were successful. In response to the communists' court case to prevent all foreign adoptions, the West Bengal government ruled to legalize them so long as the child was accompanied by an authorized adult. All the orphanages then selected countries where they had established working relationships with competent foreign agencies. The M.C. had chosen Belgium, Italy, and France, known to be Catholic-dominated countries. She told Cliff that she knew it would not be easy to get this baby, but she had faith in him and gave him her blessings again.

"You must learn to believe in miracles."

At some point, the photographs began showing a tikka on the baby's forehead. Evidently the M.C. had decided she was Hindu. Or was this Dionysia's way of discouraging interest by the Belgians? Since the law required that native Hindus adopt at least 50 percent of Bengali children, Hindus would have first choice. And we knew which sex Indians would prefer, especially given the unwritten requirement to provide a dowry for a daughter's marriage.

In Cliff's absence, I kept busy sending off for the mountain of documents needed to process the adoption, should we be so blessed as to have her someday—fully aware of the fact that India's post was as dependable as India's phones or India's electricity.

Our 14 x 10 in. foolscap file grew and grew to accommodate India's yellowing overlong paper. Documents required to complete our application for foreign appointment of guardianship were as follows: first, from the sponsoring foreign agency (Travelers Aide, Chicago), a home study report, recent family photo, marriage certificate, declaration concerning adoptive father's health along with certificate regarding medical fitness duly certified by a medical practitioner, declaration of financial status along with employer's certificate, income tax assessment orders, bank references and particulars concerning properties owned, declaration of willingness to undertake guardianship of the child, power of attorney, promise of regular reports on the state of the child, and the agency's proof of license; second, from the processing Indian agency (Missionaries of Charity, hypothetically), child study report, photographs of the child, letter of approval of the child by the foreigner, documents showing child is legally free for adoption, certificate of satisfaction that there shall be no impediment in the child's immigration into prospective adoptive parents country, bond to insure adoption within two years or repatriation at foreigner's expense. All documents must be notarized by a Notary Public.

Above and beyond all that, the home study required letters of recommendation from family and friends (six) and a priest (one), letters of willingness to adopt the child if something should happen to us (four), plus our birth and marriage certificates.

As in all of India's complexities—such as whether or not to give hand-outs to the constant stream of beggars, where to get fresh milk other than from the early morning cow, what hours of the day might we count on electricity, however shall we get a telephone installed—we sought the wisdom and advice of our neighbor Kavery. As a banker and philanthropist, she seemed to be either related or connected in some way to everyone in Bangalore. She recommended a lawyer friend who recommended a social worker who would

evaluate our fitness for parenthood and then recommend us
to the Indian government. Thus our quest, requiring untold
reams of paper, was launched on what I could only describe
as an endless series of tests—some involving our patience
and endurance, others our faith, even our sincerity, and some
tests so mysterious we didn't realize we were taking them
at the time.

Our social worker was a lovely Sikh woman, Sarina,
mother of two bright children, a little girl and boy. She and
her husband had been trained at an Ivy League college in
the U.S. We were made to feel comfortable with them by
their familiarity with our American roots and by the social
routine she organized to learn about us. There were weekly
visits to and fro over breakfast, lunch, tea-time, and dinner.
Mainly I was spending a lot of time with her in my house
or hers.

Then came the evening with our husbands around her
dining room table. The children were sent off to bed. We
were well into the fourth course and the second bottle of
wine, comparing Indian and American politics to no one's
advantage. Cliff was seated at the table across from Sarina.
He tells the story like this:

"Sometime during our boring discussion, I felt something
on my leg and realized it was Sarina's foot. At first I assumed
she was just crossing her legs and, being rather long-legged,
she inadvertently brushed my leg.

"When it happened a second time with a distinct stroking
motion up and down my ankle, I knew it was intentional. At
the time, I thought she might be teasing me just to see my
reaction. I am sure my eyes showed my alarm, but I struggled
to keep a straight face. Even though it was arousing, I did not

take it as an overture but rather a mischievous act to relieve the tedium of the political discussion that our spouses were deeply engaged in. Later on it occurred to me that Sarina might have been questioning my devotion to Bonnie, which would surely have an effect on our eligibility as adoptive parents."

Cliff chose not to share the experience with me, perhaps because he had great respect for Sarina and her family. Also he knew how close she and I had become over so many months of life-and-soul-searching. She had grown to be my most intimate confidante. What could have motivated this apparent flirtation? Months later he recalled the event when we felt our sincerity and fitness to be M.C. adoptive parents were being tested.

~

March arrived with what seemed like a break-through. I read in *Deccan Herald* that Mother was planning to open a home for the destitute in Singapore, of all places. Why would wealthy, clean, and green Singapore need a Catholic Missionaries of Charity-styled home? On exactly the same day, I received an urgent cable through Cliff's BEML address from Muriel at the *Straits Times*:

84 581 78 BEMM IN
TIMESSE RS 21239
02 MAR 85
BONNIE RICHESON
INDIA
NEED YOU TO INTERVIEW MOTHER TERESA,
MISSIONARIES OF CHARITY 54/A LOWER

CIRCULAR ROAD, CALCUTTA 700016 ASAP. WE HAVE ST STORY THAT SHE MAY SET UP HOME FOR POOR AND DESTITUTE IN S'PORE. WHEN IS SHE COMING TO DISCUSS PLANS? WHY IS SHE DOING THIS? HOW CAN HER ORGANISATION CONTRIBUTE TO AFFLUENT URBANISED SOCI-ETIES WHEN POOR AND NEEDY DO NOT HAVE SUCH OBVIOUS PROFILE AS IN INDIA? ETC.ETC. LETTER FOLLOWS. REGARDS MURIEL SPEEDEN, ASSISTANT TO THE EDITOR, SECTION TWO STRAITS TIMES, SINGAPORE.

I knew *The Straits Times* staff had not forgotten me, had not forgotten the importance of that shared experience at Darjeeling. Muriel had been with me when we found Pema, and now here she was coming to the rescue, armed with a real assignment guaranteed to culminate in our meeting Mother Teresa herself. Fast as I could, I couriered a request for an interview with Mother.

17 Grant Road Cross
Bangalore 560 001
4 March, 1985

Mother Teresa
Missionaries of Charity
54/A Lower Circular Road
Calcutta700 016

Dear Reverend Mother,
    The Straits Times *of Singapore sent a telex received today asking that I interview you regarding the Missionaries of Charity*

home proposed for Singapore. For your reference, I enclose a copy of that communication and the announcement that appeared in the Singapore newspaper on 18 January, 1985.

I would like to introduce myself briefly. I am an American writer living in Bangalore over the last year, transplanted from a three-year spell in Singapore. There I wrote features for The Straits Times *and continue to enjoy a good association with the editors. (See bio-data enclosed.)*

Both the newspaper staff and the people of Singapore are keen to know more from you about your objectives there. Thus the urgent telex requesting that I see you as soon as possible. However, I am aware of the Christian commitment that fills your schedule and frequently takes you away from Calcutta.

Is it possible for me to meet with you in Calcutta sometime between now and the end of March. I need only enough notice of appointment to buy an Air India ticket and catch the night flight from Bangalore to Calcutta. I should mention that we plan to leave for the states early April to visit with our families on our annual one-month home leave.

Beyond the professional assignment, there is a matter of great personal importance to myself and my husband I would like to discuss with you. I look forward to hearing from you with great anticipation.

May this letter find you blessed with the strength of health to match your purpose.

Most sincerely,
Bonnie Tinsley-Richeson

Encls: as indicated

Now in hindsight, I must confess that I had little hope of receiving the response I most wanted. I did what I thought

Pema and Cliff at Calcutta orphanage

I should have done in writing the letter, even though I knew that being honest about both the controversial nature of the news story and my underlying purpose in writing, i.e., to get the baby, would bar any success of an interview with Mother Teresa. And the letter was way too long for someone with her workload, who answered her own mail and woke up every morning with a fever—I only found out later. I was prepared for disappointment. I was anxious to get home. There would be more time to figure out the next step when we returned to India, unless of course this was my one and only hope of ever meeting her. I had not forgotten Shashi and Minu's advice. It was essential to get to Mother herself.

The days and nights that followed in waiting for her response were taken up with fantasies of that meeting. Did I even dare to dream it, being in the powerful presence of that saintly woman, more filled with the Holy Spirit than the Pope, at least to my mind? I had seen her so often in magazines and newspapers that I had memorized practically every crevice of that world-wizened face, always uplifted as if to hear better her instructions from above. This could be the most important interview of my life. This could be the most important moment of my life.

After two weeks without a reply from her, I cabled the following:

TO FOLLOW UP MY LETTER OF 4 MARCH, MAY I HAVE A HALF HOUR OF YOUR TIME BETWEEN NOW AND APRIL 1. IF SO, PLEASE NAME THE DATE IN PAID REPLY. NO SUCCESS REACH- ING YOU BY PHONE. FAITHFULLY, BONNIE TINSLEY-RICHESON.

Her reply arrived in Bangalore on 27 March:

BONNIE TINSLEY RICHESON17 GRANTROADCROSSBANGALORE560001 X1705LA198CALCUTTAP2614 — NOT POSSIBLE —KOTHER TERESA [sic]

Chapter 12

HOME LEAVE

E*ven if we cannot have Pema now or ever, I pack photos of her to show off to family and friends on our annual return home. The pictures are a poor substitute. I want everyone actually to see her to believe her, maybe believe in this make-believe mother too.*

~

In April, we planned to return to the States on home leave through Bombay. Before we could leave India, we had to acquire an exit visa, officially called "a no objection to leave tax clearance," a form of bond promising to return, or in the event that we did not, surrender all our household belongings. To ease the path to residence, we had entered India not on a business visa, the normal but time-consuming route, but on a "transfer of residence" visa. In other words, to avoid all the paperwork required to enter and leave India every few months on a business visa, we had immigrated to India. There was no problem getting into India. The question now was whether or not we would be able to get out of India.

We had to have permission not only from Bangalore police but also the income tax and customs folks. And as in all Indian matters governmental, no one really seemed to be sure exactly about procedures—this most knowledgeable official or that one was on leave, or out of station, or lost and never to be found, and so we will spend the rest of our lives running from one scrap of information to another, never getting the whole story. So far we managed to tolerate most of dear ole India's vagaries and mananas, but when it was a matter of *going home*, or a

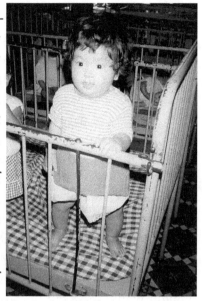

Pema at Calcutta orphanage, Shishu Bhavan

matter of personal freedom and movement, I felt like I had to shake the very gates of Hell.

Well, as it turned out on my umpteenth visit to the local Customs office, the man who knew about such complicated matters was "out of station" (which always suggests to me the status of a missing person), so I got shuffled down a maze of musty, gray-stained corridors lined with stacks of tattered paper that reminded me more of shelves cluttered with dirty laundry, a suspender dangling here, a bra-strap there, ragged something or the others. I was ushered into this room where two men with furrowed brows were debating the proper procedure, neither one willing to admit he did not know, and of course the recommended course of action involved a trip to Madras or Bombay or Delhi where the Collector of Customs, nameless and perhaps also a missing person, would surely know what to do. It was suggested that I might write a letter to the nameless Collector. Now, mind you, it was our plan to leave no later than the coming weekend and already they have stretched our departure until at least 1986. I have passed the blunt edge of despair and am now on the verge of tears, a small river forming which I dam up in my throat until I get home for Cliff to receive the full overflow.

~

Finally the day did arrive for our departure from India to the States. We managed to reach Bombay with bags packed and air tickets in hand on April 18. At Bombay's Citibank, Ravi Batia, the young western-educated manager dressed in loafers and oxford cloth, handed us the documents he thought would serve our purpose.

"There are so few Americans trying to get in and out of India these days," he said, "I'm not sure this is what you need. But there are more than enough stamps on these papers to look impressively official," he grinned.

As we were driven from government office to government office, each one stacked floor to ceiling with similar bundles of documents, as we were trying to procure official signatures and collect said documents with all of Bombay's traffic converging on our line of passage, growing more congested and steamy by the hour with bicycles, auto-rickshaws, ox-drawn carts, and sacred cows wandering about, it dawned on me that we would not make our flight to D. C.

Finally, when there was yet another delay at yet another office, I could not contain my frustration any longer and broke down in tears in front of the old bureaucrat in khaki uniform behind the desk.

"Please, sir. I just need to get home to see my mother and celebrate her 70th birthday with her." Actually, I was addressing the whole room full of clerks in bright-colored sarees and barefooted messenger boys buried in dust-covered, tumble-down piles of brown paper tied up in red twine, (source of the proverbial "red tape"). One of these bundles could very well be our papers, the missing needle in the haystack. Even though no eyes were moved by my tears, hands moved with a final flourish of stamping that echoed throughout the dimly lit room, like those mysterious sounds of distress I imagined filling the Marabar Caves, and we were on our way.

When we reached Dulles Airport 20-some hours later, I cried for joy to see the tall, stately lady who was my mother. In all those months of missing her, however, I had forgotten her true nature. I longed to show her the few pictures we had of the baby and confide all my wishes and fears about motherhood. Unfortunately, my sweet mother was always one to counsel against her only child taking risks. Contact lenses would scar my eyeballs. If I had my ears pierced, I would lose my earlobes to infections. Birth-control pills would make me sterile. She lived in fear of my every disappointment, which she took personally.

~

The day I moved out of my mother's house for good, I had just turned 21. I had already lived away from home for four college years, albeit in women's dorms. But from her point of view, I was jumping ship. Since my father's departure 19 years earlier, except for his occasional Sunday visits and schooling subsidies, it had been just the two of us, mother and daughter, for better or worse, for richer or poorer, until death or a proper replacement guardian in the form of a husband should assert himself. She wasn't happy that all my church girlfriends had promptly married directly after college and I had not.

On that moving day, Mother and I sat side by side on the edge of my bed, not daring to look each other in the eye. I was focused on the open window, the end-of-summer breezes blowing the curtains, and the car-lined street just below. I told her that my college roommate Rosie and I had found an apartment close to where we worked. It was time for me to live my own life apart from my mother's and no longer in the shadow of Hawthorne. That was her given name, as elegant as the bearer. I was not elegant. Once I had escaped her full-time attention, I took up bridge and smoking to stoke my sophistication. I managed to lose the rolls of baby fat she packed me off to college with and was voted Greek queen runner-up my junior year. I had done a few other things she would not be proud of. I had stopped attending church and befriended an African-American girl at work. I would have loved to have brought Esther home for Mother's southern fried chicken but thought better of it.

If my mother was anything, it was polite, not what some call southern-veneer polite but genuinely polite. Every-one loved her for it. After all she was the product of her First-Family-of-Virginia, deeply rooted in genteel tradition. She had grown up with servants who were brown-skinned, each and every one "a treasure" to her, she vowed. But she did have her prejudices. Otherwise, she would not have sent me to private girls' schools to avoid de-segregation.

"I had no idea you felt that way," she protested without a sound that could be mistaken for anger. I was the one agitating over leaving home. I was crying. My mother was not. In fact, I never remember seeing my mother cry.

"You can go," she said, "but don't expect any more help from me or your father." That level of threat was worrying, since I had just started to work for a government task force with no firm expectation of date of payment. And I had just purchased *The Great Books of the Western World*, the entire set of 54 volumes, all leather-bound, plus the ten-volume *Gateway* set. They were already sending me notices of delayed payment.

"That's perfectly alright with me. Rosie has a good-paying job and has promised to tie me over until I get my first paycheck."

"Well, we'll see. What did you say you were wearing to Carol's wedding at the church?"

In all fairness to my mother, I should say that her protests might have had more to do with my move to Washington, D. C. and DuPont Circle, not yet the fomenting ground of youthful war rebellion and drug culture, but well on its way. Rosie had found a basement apartment in a brownstone on 17th and R Streets just down the block from the Sierra Leone embassy, which also did not sit well with my parents. Daddy did come to exchange a few cautionary words with the landlady, whose German gave him even more pause. Countess von Mandelslau had left Berlin in the arms of her American journalist lover at the end of World War II and severed ties with the Count in every way but with the title she liked. She plied us with stories of her war adventures and with German pates and pumpernickel from the corner deli. Rosie and I loved her. She had our best interests at heart. She filled the upstairs apartments with eligible, freshly graduated males from the Ivy League.

Mother never saw nor did she set foot on the premises, so far as I know.

~

My mother did not wait to leave Dulles Airport before speaking her mind.

"Don't get your hopes up, sweetheart," was her best advice in the matter of the baby. "I don't think you realize what you're getting yourself into, trying to adopt a foreigner." Then she reminded me that I was 41, probably too old for such an undertaking and by now too self-centered. She had a habit of changing the subject when she was uncomfortable and so she launched into a report about the exhibits on India at the National Gallery and the Smithsonian. She would not be going but she knew that Cliff and I would want to see them.

Again, here was proof of the India fever overtaking the U.S. The Festival of India on the Mall was in full swing with all the sights, sounds, and smells typical of an Indian fair or *mela*. At the National Gallery of Art, a breathtaking exhibit of India's ancient sculpture in stone, bronze, and ivory had arrived like a magic caravan blown in from the East. A thrill passed through me as I entered the carved gateway of Sanchi's Great Stupa in photomural framing the entrance to the exhibit. There, in reverent half-light, the sculptures were aglow with life, each one basking under a halo of soft light to fully reveal the object's beauty and fine workmanship.

Plump-bellied Ganesha with trunk a-sway, Shiva gesturing with all eight arms, amorous couples entwined, serpents twisting, celestial creatures in flight—the unique pantheon seemed to emanate energy, both physical and spiritual. Indeed the whole show danced, as one critic so aptly described it. In the respectful quiet, you could almost hear the strains of a morning raga—the sitar, the tabla, the Indian flute.

Our friends and family in the D.C. area somehow had the notion that we were living the life of the colonial British in some Technicolor splendor. Actually we live, the sole American family in a neighborhood of Hindus, Muslims, and Christians of all skin tones, all speaking a musical ensemble of Indian languages that harmonize well enough with American-styled English. No, we explained, we do not live in an American expat compound surrounded by our countrymen and conveniences. Now and again we can get imported bottled mineral water, but the cost is too dear to buy regularly. Therefore every morning, if there is electricity, I have to boil our drinking water. I have a stainless steel tank with two chalk filters, plus a carbon filter on the main spigot. My routine is to boil the day's supply and then pour it in the top of this tank, about two gallons or so, which works well enough except the filters clog too fast with India's muddy water and I have to start all over again boiling more water to sterilize the system. I do constant battle with the boiling and the filtering but am glad for it so long as there is water, even a dribble through the tap. There are frequent periods of drought bad enough in themselves but worse when they are accompanied by cholera outbreaks.

Along with the water, I have to boil the milk, since it comes directly from a cow announced by her tinkle-tinkle, delivered at our front gate, and therefore not pasteurized. Despite the cheery face on the cow and her farmer, the lovely white liquid she dispenses into the bucket is contaminated with deadly organisms putting us at risk for typhoid fever, tuberculosis, diphtheria, and a host of other life-threatening diseases. Boiling milk requires great concentration. I must have let it boil over umpteen hundreds of times, and there is no more god-awful mess to clean off an electric burner than fresh milk. For all that time and trouble, however, I must say we shall probably never taste such delicious curds again.

So why do I perform all this labor myself when everyone knows servants are so cheap in India. As a matter of fact, we do have a part-time cleaning lady or *ayah*, whose name is Kamala, on loan from our neighbor Kavery. But I am not about to trust Kamala with our water or milk when her method of washing dishes is to use sand from the garden where the cats have peed. Even after I explained with the help of Tamil interpreters all the hygienic reasons for using detergent instead of sand, I would catch her returning to her old ways. She also had trouble distinguishing the cloth used on the floor from the cloth used on the dishes. Even our most well-informed neighbors (i.e., the ones well-traveled or educated in the west) seem to lack any sort of standard of kitchen hygiene but leave their stomachs, as well as their souls, to the gods, be they microscopic. In all matters of health, I refer regularly to my copy of the Peace Corps Manual of 3rd world survival, *Where There Is No Doctor.*

Before I was wizened to the ways of India, I used to think that all those piles of dung hardening on the streets were livestock inspired. Then on one of my early morning walks around Cubbon Park, I noticed a man immaculately clad all in white from the little crocheted cap on his head down to his skirted feet. He looked to be kneeling by the side of the road, his face averted from the busy thoroughfare, turned toward Mecca in proper position for his morning prayers. When I got within nose range of him, however, I realized what he was up to. My neighbor Kavery was always complaining about these "misuses of the premises."

We do not have "servants." For the sake of company security, we have a small group of loyal employees, who are respected and rewarded for their hard work. Muthuswamy is Cliff's driver, Balraj is the head watchman, James handles the night duty, and Muniyappa is the *mali,* that's the gardener, whose uniform is a shawl and loin-cloth. He gets his feelings hurt if I revise his planting scheme in any way. His special gift is spotting cobras inside our compound walls. This he reports faithfully to Balraj, who in turn reports it to me. No one dares raise the issue with the boss, the Sahib. It is understood that Cliff's deathly fear of snakes must be respected, since it hearkens back to his Irish roots.

In the matter of food, I have to wash all our fruits and vegetables in puritabs. A cloud of flies partially envelopes the one-and-only meat market where I take my business. Inevitably there is this kilometer-long queue, so by the time I purchase my few packets (mostly still feathery lumps of chicken; the quality of beef is wanting in a predominantly Hindu country), I feel as though I have just been served up to the flies. But the proprietor is kind, a dear old Muslim grandpa whose main concern is my lack of fertility. On each visit, he inquires after my "health."

In fact, it seems like everyone in Bangalore who knows us, even peripherally, has taken an interest in my lack of fertility, even Balraj our watchman. We were on a recent trip to Mysore, famous for its "city of palaces" with great bulbous turrets and scalloped windows in the Mogul tradition about two to three hours' drive from Bangalore. Balraj, as self-appointed guide, made a point of taking us down a long, winding road to some vague tourist destination. After what felt like too long, we came upon a huge single piece of stone carved in the shape of a very round, black, and gently smiling bull, the Nandi of Hindu mythology. By Indian standards, this was a small shrine cut into a small mountain, so only one white-robed and shaven priest presided. In the shade of a tall fern-leaf tree, a half-dozen bulls dozed and occasionally worried a pesky fly with their tails. Round cow patties were baking on the side of a boulder. Four mama monkeys and their tiny bald charges were lined up casually near the entrance.

Standing next to the sleepy-eyed bull, I am given a yellow flower and a vermilion dot in mid-forehead (this, to ward off evil eyes) and then I am told to make a wish and crawl under Nandi's left foreleg. Even though it is a squeeze at the hip-line, I pass through and we are on intimate terms now, the bull and I. When Balraj tells me that Nandi is "oh, so very old" and believed to be actually growing, I do not dispute his word. I don't even ask how old. Perhaps truth in India is only in the moment or a matter of personal preference in the mind of the believer. And when the plumber says he will return soon with the proper tools, he is only in the moment of believing, which most probably will linger until he is pedaling away on his bike to the next job or coffee break.

~

One of the deprivations we suffer most or least, depending on how you look at it, is the absence of a telephone. Either the wheels of government communications run understandably slow or we have failed sufficiently to grease the right palm. On the occasions when I have to use our neighbor Kavery's phone, I learn again that we are blessed to be without one.

Reaching and then maintaining any connection could only be described as an exercise in frustration, especially with all the hello-hello-helloing that seems essential to the process. First you start out with this litany of hellos that you keep up until something like an answer comes from the other end. Every pause in the conversation thereafter requires more hellos, just in case you have a fading connection. Somehow all those hellos have the power to revive it. It goes something like this:

"Hello, hello, hello, Bombay calling Mr. Clifford Richeson, hello, hello, hello, yes, my good sir, I am representative of The International Association Body for the Expeditious Evacuation and Prevention of Piles, hello, hello, hello, I am, to be exact, the additional deputy executive secretary, Banerji here speaking, hello, hello, hello, good sir, yes, I am calling about the matter of a solicitation, hello, hello, hello, yes, a donation. Our most worthy and esteemed patrons submit generously in amounts of ten thousand rupees, hello, hello, hello...."

Everyone asks us about elephants. Elephants are found mostly in the nature reserves, except when the Maharaja of Mysore takes a notion to throw a parade and ride his elephant all decked out trunk to toe in garlands of marigold and ceremonial vestments of silk and solid gold. Sometimes we have to compete with the monkeys for the ripe mangoes. Street musicians drumming and tooting, bullock-drawn carts with silver bells a-jangle, milk-cows, holy men, and certified rag-pickers all pass down our street and then up again since the street doesn't go anywhere, and so there is this constant parade. In fact, that pretty well describes India, such a vast country and so various with so many people who seem always to be out there no matter the time of day.

No, our car is not imported; it's India's own Ambassador model right out of the Keystone Cops era, hopelessly antique in design, but Muthuswamy expertly drives us around in it and repairs it when it breaks down. I do wonder if his constant application of the horn (standard routine with drivers) will ever dim in my ears. Oh yes, jeans are a common enough form of dress, and American pop music wafts out of cassette players.

~

When I reached Illinois and my old circle of friends, life returned to business as usual. Talk of adopting a baby in India was superseded by our trip down memory lane and a replay of all those old passions that united us. Fellow poets, members of our poetry collective, organized an overnight at a friend's house on the lake where we sat around a picnic table with wine glasses in hand until nearly daylight. These were women with no interest whatsoever in children, either because they had no children, had already had their children, and/or were totally involved in their careers. It was easy to fall into the old camaraderie with them.

At that inevitable turning point in the night made too long with drinking, one of my best friends on the art faculty at the University turned to me and said, "What DO you do?" I was speechless for a moment. Was the question meant to dig at my lack of full-time employment, which I left to follow Cliff, who was now my sole source of support?

Where would I begin to tell about my life in India and my work which was a part of that? I would have to have the time to unravel this strange world of monkeys in the mango trees and black-draped women in *purdah*, hours spent in kitchen and household tedium because the part-time staff's standards of hygiene fell far short of mine, hours spent helping Cliff through another work crisis, underlying this, the pretty constant anxiety about his safety. All the while I am searching for and recording as best I can in words the beauty and truth of this place so that our time here will not have been wasted.

My tendency is to shy away from talk about myself unless, of course, there is a problem that needs a faithful ear. What I do in India, while keeping up with Singapore and stateside writing, what I've managed to accomplish in a short residence may not sound like much. I took on program chair for the American and Overseas Women's Club and fund-raising for the "street-school" we support in the worst of Bangalore's slums. I go there to help out one day a week. On my desk to answer: an invitation to write a history-guide for the Lal Bagh Gardens here similar to *Singapore Green*, another invitation to work as consultant with The Indian National Trust for Art and Cultural Heritage (that's the body responsible for The Festival of India now in the U.S.), plus two lectures on tropical plants to work up. These did not come to me by sitting around twiddling my thumbs. And should I mention the movie, *Bettada Hoovu* (Hill Flower), in which I had a small walk-on part, or rather drive-on part. I got to play the part of my American self as a mother driving her two children somewhere. In fact, I was driving my friend Marcia Jamal's children, Adi and Mushtaq. Cliff said I was a "lead action character" but Marcia was the one with the leading role. She played the part of an American woman living in India who befriends a poor village boy.

I was just thrilled to be able to drive a car again. It was a sporty-looking Sterling, a British-made car brought into India at the request of some higher-ups in government and a huge improvement over the boxy Ambassador. I was hoping that the scene would require several takes so that I would have lots of experience behind the wheel. No such luck. The Director was satisfied with the first take. Following that, I was asked to write about the movie for *SPAN*, the magazine published by the U. S. Information Service in New Delhi to bridge relations between India and America. And *SPAN* had also commissioned an article about the India exhibit at the Smithsonian which was due on my return to India.

Perhaps it is peculiar to this achievement-oriented generation of American women that what I DO, all these damned gold stars, has come to be the measure of who I am, and if I am not at the full pitch of action or laid up from the exhaustion of overwork, then I am somehow diminished as a person. The question of "What DO you do?" suggested that. In truth, I may have been coming under the influence of the strong, yet gentle women of India whose culture I was coming to know and appreciate. More and more I saw the sanity in BEING the person I am (as long as she stays loving and human!), just myself and letting the life and work left to me evolve out of that, rather than chasing after more gold stars. In a word, my audience that night wasn't interested in baby talk.

~

There was definitely more encouragement from Cliff's family, practicing Catholics all. Sister-in-law Denise had borne three future soccer players already. She would have completed the team had Cliff's brother Bob been agreeable. Their blond and athletic good looks, when lined up in front of their Winnebago camper, went a long way in selling the campers, which was Bob's current work. They had drafted a letter, properly stamped and notarized, promising to adopt the baby if ever "something should happen to the adoptive parents."

Not until we reached Dubuque and Dorothy, my best friend since grad school days at Iowa, did I get back on track with my mission. Over preparations in her kitchen for the chicken curry I had been longing to share with friends, she plied me with questions about this baby and gave the kind of encouragement I needed. Dorothy's daughter Jenny took a long whiff of the spicy kitchen air during our elaborate preparations and rushed to the telephone to invite her girlfriends.

"We can stretch it to feed three more, can't we," Jenny tossed off on the way upstairs to put on her new Punjabi-styled chemise and *churidar* pajamas I had brought her for a "show and tell."

"Oh, sure," Dorothy winked at me. I was praying the rice would grow a little in the pot. In the end, the *rasam* was a bit too spicy for the girls' tender palates. As discussion warmed around the table, the peppery *rasam* and over-spiced curries cooled on their plates.

The fact that Dorothy, too, was Catholic and had a fervent respect for Mother Teresa may have helped increase her enthusiasm for our cause. Oddly enough, I had forgotten, but Cliff reminded me of something Dorothy had said some years ago when she learned we would most probably be posted to India.

"Mother Teresa lives in India. Maybe she will help you find a baby."

Like Sister Dionysia, Dorothy sent me on my way with a renewed faith in myself and my mothering capabilities.

Chapter 13
TO CALCUTTA WITH LOVE

In an effort to calm my anxiety, I commit to memory the quote from St. Teresa on the chapel wall at Tindharia, "Everything is grace, for everything is God's gift......To the heart that loves all is well." Our hearts cannot have been more full of love for that tiny one in Sr. Dionysia's care. Our love will overcome every obstacle on our way to her, and all will be well. Still I cannot help thinking that Narayan Godbole, Forster's inscrutable Brahmin philosopher, would have a different take on the outcome. Treating the guests at Fielding's gathering to a raga, Godbole sings a religious song summoning the aid of the god Krishna. The Lord of the Universe refuses to come to him. Even after innumerable pleas, the god refuses to come.

"I say to Him, Come, come, come, come, come, come. He neglects to come."

~

By the end of August 1985, Cliff and I were making plans to go back together to the Himalayan foothills to visit with the baby and Sister Dionysia at the Tindharia orphanage, to seek the advice of our one true supporter in the M.C. organization—all in preparation for another return trip to the

Motherhouse at Calcutta in the vain hope of seeing Mother Teresa. Early in the week another telex had come from *The Straits Times* summoning me to interview Mother again. So far, my every attempt to interview Mother had been met with resistance. Her organization could see through our feeble tactics. At that point, nine months into the wait, I felt that I had had enough time and distance on the decision. I must fight or give it up.

We arrived at Tindharia late in the afternoon. Sister Dionysia and her staff remembered us even from ten months ago, and we felt so welcome there. She took us upstairs where about 20 little ones were sitting neatly on a long table about to get a feeding. She asked us to pick out our baby. I saw her immediately, as soon as I entered the room. She seemed to shine out over the rest of the children, but I took my time and made a show of looking and there was this question—how could she be so beautiful, that tiny charcoal-smeared face I had carried with me since our first Darjeeling visit, blinking wonder at us like a rosy-cheeked China doll?

She was sick again with diarrhea, a little feverish, and kept dozing off in our arms. But we held her and held her for hours that felt like minutes until the rains came with the dark and we knew we had to get up the mountain to Darjeeling. At some point Sister Dionysia slipped away into the little chapel. Later we found out she was praying for us to somehow have that baby knowing full well from Calcutta authorities it was next to impossible.

We did the two-hour climb from Tindharia to Darjeeling in heavy rains and flashes of lightening so close they seemed to send sparks off rocks. We picked up a stranded couple on the way, and the conversation helped relieve the questions and doubts in our heads, not doubts about our feelings but doubts about hurdles in Calcutta. The staff was waiting for us at the Windamere. Supper was a feast, as usual. They built a fire in a newly cemented fireplace, so the stuff popped and spewed and exploded off and on until we gave up dodging the flying sparks and wood chips and went to bed.

On Sunday we spent the afternoon with the children and Sisters up on the hill at Shanta Bhavan and then found Pema's shop open. We bought a prayer wheel for Cliff, a necklace for a friend in the States, a wooden block that prints prayer flags for me, and a bracelet shaped with the letters "Om Mani Padme Hum," the Tibetan Buddhist mantra of great compassion. Then we were down the hill to Amala and her younger daughter Yeshi and so much laughter and chatter and holding on to each other that I knew with so much hope filling Amala's room the baby would come to us. Amala was wearing a very tough brace, a leather contraption of straps and boards, which she vowed gave her back relief.

Darjeeling was just as beautiful in early September with the rains heavy on the vines so thick they seemed to cover the mountain like spider webs draped over forgotten treasures in vast ancient rooms. I hadn't remembered so much forest. How could we take the baby from this beautiful part of the world, I kept thinking until I remembered that she probably rarely saw anything outside the orphanage walls. The Sisters were being very careful to keep them undercover from the lung infections that often lead to TB.

We never saw Kanchenjunga in its fullness due to the heavy fog that kept drifting in and out of our windows, but the hot-water-bottle warmed our aching feet and the whole place felt like home, like the Warm Springs, Virginia of my childhood. I still can picture my grandmother drying my socks over a wood stove in the kitchen smelling of fresh-picked apples and cinnamon and then climbing to the four -posted feather bed in damp musty sheets that fold you down in mountain comfort, down to quiet, and you sleep better because the air is lighter, fresher. Guess I love Darjeeling much the way I loved that Shenandoah Valley home which isn't home anymore, except in the memory.

Early Monday morning we left Darjeeling with a boxed breakfast. Pema, the shop-keeper, and Yeshi were at the hotel to say goodbye, wrapping us in the white ceremonial *khata* scarves traditional with Tibetan send-offs. At the Tindharia orphanage, we held the baby and spooned her breakfast. Reluctantly we had to leave to reach Bagdogra in time for our flight to Calcutta. Thank God the fever was gone and her appetite had returned. She seemed livelier with food and quite healthy-looking with bright, inquisitive eyes, but not quite trusting those eyes. She had a little cough she stifled. I wondered if they might be feeding her too much. She wasn't trying to stand up. Again, we felt the urgency to have her with us soon.

~

Tuesday morning we reach Mother's office in Calcutta and she is IN, so says the tiny hand-painted sign over the long chain that rings the bell. We pull on the chain. The big wooden doors open at once. A young, sweet-faced Indian nun takes us to an official-looking waiting room and we settle down among the paintings of Jesus, photos of Pope John Paul II, and poster words of encouragement. All around us young girls in sarees are scrubbing the floors.

First we have to give our request on a small slip of paper.

Then we are told that Mother has a fever and can't see us but would like a letter stating exactly what we have come for. So I write the letter as simply as I can, remembering Dionysia saying that she is a simple and direct person, and tell it plain. I hand it over to the little postulate from Tamil Nadu, who bows and hurries off. What feels like hours later, we get the letter returned with a note to Sister Margaret Mary: "Please see to this couple—how to help them to get the baby. MT"

So we rush off to Sister Margaret Mary again, trusting fools that we are, and just like nine months ago she says no again. I have this flash of a terrible dream of some vague injustice at the hands of someone unfeeling and I am doomed to keep repeating my efforts until frustration spends me. She tells us that Mother is sick and doesn't understand our situation, that she is authorized to give babies only to Belgium, Italy, and France, finished!

We return to the hotel. Cliff collapses on the couch. I can't believe the sadness I see in my face, like an old woman in the mirror. How to describe the hours that seemed like days of despair when we had no one to turn to, when we were so discouraged we were beyond thinking our way through to the next step—and what step? It felt like Calcutta, that whole city of human waste and utter squalor, all of it was concentrated in our miserable hotel room. What was worse, we were powerless to help each other drifting deeper and deeper into our separate sorrows.

I don't know what shook me awake enough to call the American Consulate, even against Cliff's criticism of the quality of services they perform. But I went ahead screaming like a fishwife into the phone to be understood, just like trying to talk long-distance to Singapore. I manage to make an appointment to get a notary stamp on one of the adoption documents.

By 5:00 pm we reach the Consulate where we share our sad story with the Notary Public. She summons the Consul himself, an ex-marine with the bearing of a man still in uniform but who speaks with the greatest tenderness and compassion. Louis Anthony McCall's caring, informed advice turns us around toward hope. I can't believe how knowledge-able and sympathetic this man is. From him we gather that Missionaries of Charity has had a history of bad feelings attached to American adoptions. Rumor has it that Mother stopped giving babies to Americans because of some awful scandal involving an agency that was shipping newborns like factory products from India to the U. S. in the care of airline stewardesses. One 3-month-old baby died on route. But he let us know that Mother was the one to have the last word, no one else.

"Mother is tough as nails," he told us confidentially, "but really a sweet old lady. If you hope to see her in person, you should go to the Motherhouse at vespers." It was her practice to attend adoration before vespers and then welcome visitors during the next hour. Because of the mammoth size of her charitable outreach, it was customary for visitors to bring money or gifts to support her work caring for the world's poorest of the poor.

"She will have to see you if you are there," the ex-Marine grinned at us and shook Cliff's hand. "I have the feeling she will help you. Remember, she's a mother. Approach her like a mother." We got the message. Go back to Mother. Now.

Chapter 14

THE LAST HOPE

E*arlier in the day we go to the Mission of Hope, an American agency that deals with Calcutta adoptions, just to find out if there might be some way they can get the baby for us. Again the woman in charge is in the States. Every time we go there she's been in the States. Next week maybe she will return. And more than ever we're feeling the urgency to get this baby. At some point, Cliff asks what if she has to grow up in this place. Indeed that seems possible. Maybe the Belgian families want only "perfect" children, remembering the bluish birthmarks which almost cover her back and legs. I don't look carefully. There seems no reason to, but the marks are on her tiny arms as well.*

~

It was 6:00 pm. The line of visitors snaked from far down Calcutta's mean streets, past pavement shops and smoky food stalls, past ragged squatters and beggars, past open drains knee-deep in garbage and fetid water from the recent monsoon, all the way to Lower Circular Road and the entrance here at the narrow cul-de-sac into the three-story building, the Motherhouse. The line looked interminable, as all Indian queues do. This one was notable, however, in that everyone was carrying a plastic bag with the British retailer WH Smith travel store logo. British pilgrims, I thought, bringing their gifts to her.

In the Indian custom of total disregard for first-come-first-serve, Cliff and I broke the queue and entered the tiny courtyard to muffled protests. A cooling hush replaced the deafening noise outside. It was too dark to see anything beyond the sea of shiny plastic WH Smith bags full of children's books, clothes, and toys. Suddenly I felt a tug at my sleeve. The same young postulate who had befriended us earlier in the day beckoned us to follow her toward the back of the Motherhouse to a narrow set of iron stairs.

"What should I say to Mother?" I whispered to her, pleading for instruction.

"Just tell her about your love. She will understand a mother's love." Then she motioned us to climb the stairs while she waited below.

At the top we saw a landing dimly lit and a sort of bridge filled with another sea of tourists. In the half light, I could make out a door, perhaps to an office in the far distance toward which the bridge was leading and empty space falling off both sides of the wooden bridge edged by metal railings. Tourists were massing toward her, someone said from Liverpool. A small Indian delegation with cameras stood to her left. I could just barely see her behind all that. She looked so weary. I guess she had to follow her routine, if she was at all able.

In the vain hope of actually meeting with her, I had been following news of her activities and her health history in the *Deccan Herald*—or as much information as her organization would give out. Even after being diagnosed in 1983 with a serious heart condition, discovered providentially when she fell from her bed while on a visit to Pope John Paul II in Rome, she had kept up the usual intensity of her activity. She continued to establish numerous foundations all over the world, including the growth of male branches of her religious family. In October 1984 she formed the first Missionaries of Charity Fathers in New York. And in December of the same year her punishing schedule included an emergency visit to the victims of the Bhopal factory disaster in Madhya Pradesh, in spite of the health risks to her and the Sisters accompanying her.

Probably the most publicized event took place January 1985 in Ethiopia's Addis Ababa airport. Her unexpected encounter with pop star Bob Geldof gave them the opportunity to compare notes on charity work both were doing in Africa. Geldof was there to spend the millions his Band Aid concert had raised. Mother was there to persuade a government minister to give her two old abandoned buildings for her orphanages. Confident in the power of her urgent requests, she immediately sent a message for assistance directly to President Reagan. He responded with a gift of aid to Ethiopia in the amount of US $64 million. His personal letter to Mother followed, expressing his doubt that the money would reach the people who needed it.

In May, just a few months ago, she was again in the U. S. to receive the Presidential Medal of Freedom from President Reagan. At that time she set up a hospice for AIDS victims in Greenwich Village and then traveled to China to commend Deng Pufang, the wheelchair-bound son of Premier Deng Xiaoping, for his program to aid the handicapped. Clearly all these cross-continental activities were taking their toll.

Her strength was failing and she was never long without sickness and pain.

~

At the top of the steps of the Motherhouse and still behind so many masses waiting in line to see her, I think to myself this is impossible. There are too many. Why do we keep fooling ourselves? It will take a miracle to reach her. By the time we do, she will have given out, if she is as ill as they insist she is. I was about to turn around and go back down the stairs when I feel a pressure on my left shoulder, like a warm hand. It is not Cliff's. He is standing close on my right. There is no one, just a voice behind me gently repeating, "Wait, wait." I look to see who might have spoken to me. There was no one there. For this, I have no explanation.

Soon enough we were with her in the half-light. There was a break in the line of tourists, like the Red Sea parting. The Indian delegation moved away to the side. Finally we were standing in front of Mother Teresa herself. Since I had given up any hope of ever seeing her in person many months ago, I did not know what to expect. There was this powerful feeling of accessibility, in spite of the weight of her reputation which should have been off-putting. She was totally present for us.

She stood just an inch above my shoulder and a little stooped over. Although from a distance she looked so frail and small, close up she held to a sturdiness that belied her years and her heart condition. At first it was hard to read her face, tanned and deeply weathered. Did she know about us and how desperately we were trying to adopt the baby in her care? Was she going to be as stubborn as those in her organization in charge of adoptions? And was she also trying to avoid us?

Then she smiled, pulled us toward her with her strong hands and told us that she knew our story.

"You know," she said, "how can I in good conscience give you this baby when I have said no to so many other Americans? It doesn't seem fair, does it?"

We—no—I began to argue with the fervency of the true mother standing before King Solomon. Fear made me cold as ice, but desperation heated my words to her. I told her how we loved that baby as soon as we laid eyes on her and held her in our arms ten months ago when she was only ten days old in Darjeeling (the very place Mother began her novitiate, took her first and final vows, and where she was headed on a train when she heard God's call to Calcutta's poorest of the poor!), how we had done everything in our power to have her, everything required by both the Indian and U.S. governments to complete the necessary paperwork, including many more letters of recommendation from influential people than were required, that we lived here in India and that there should be some exceptions made for people like us. Surely she could read our hearts. Surely she could see the gaping hole in our hearts that only this baby could fill. Or something to that effect.

I was having a hard time finding the exact words while holding back the tears. In the midst of my long disjointed, emotional outburst, Cliff moved forward. Mother let go of my cold hands and took his. While he spoke as convincingly as he could about his feelings, she was stroking the hair on his forearm as if to sooth him. But through her tenderness, I could see that this woman meant business. She had rules and we were breaking them. We were not Catholic, this was not my first marriage, and we were Americans.

I can't recall how long the conversation lasted. I was glad that Cliff had the last word. Mother seemed to be especially responsive to him. I kept thinking we were taking up more than our un-allotted time, and we had no gifts for her. But I can say that in those brief moments, secure in the strength of her embrace, I felt I had known this woman all my life or that she had known me, intimately, like a beloved aunt or teacher. I want to say that her gaze was penetrating, that I felt her take her time to look all the way through my faults and self-doubts and come out on the other side to wrap me in her all-inclusive acceptance, judgement-free. Yes, to me she was "Mother Teresa," bearing the full force of that godly name and reputation.

Also, she bore the human face of motherly compassion that had witnessed first-hand the pain and suffering, the squalor and sub-human conditions of the outcasts, the lepers, the terminally ill and dying, those the rest of the world had abandoned.

"I must pray about this," she said, letting go of Cliff's hand. "Come to my office first thing in the morning, and I'll give you my answer."

"What time?"

"Come at 7:30. I will pray, and you pray too."

And she turned her smile on the ones behind us with the WH Smith bags. It was odd that standing just next to her I was oblivious to everything and everyone around us, all those lines of people from Liverpool, unaware of everything but Mother and her strong, warm hands pulling me toward her and pushing me away. By the curious look on their faces, I was aware that time had stopped also for those visitors standing behind us. They all seemed to be waiting patiently, quiet, and respectful, as if word had traveled down the line. This couple had special need of Mother Teresa. They may not be Calcutta's destitute and dying, but they were certainly needy.

We returned to the hotel and had an early supper mostly in silence. The *naan* was burned and even the mulligatawny soup tasted bitter. I guess we had reached the point of turning on each other in this long, hopeless crusade, since we were powerless to control the outside forces against us. That night Mother joined me in my restless sleep. We were locked in some form of combat, or making and remaking the bed, I can't be sure. Her white habit and the sheets kept getting confused. Inside my bed-sheets and her trade-mark white saree with the blue striped border, the small cross, and rosary at the shoulder, she and I were tumbling over and over and over.

Chapter 15

THE GOOD NEWS

$\mathcal{A}$*fter yesterday, digging my heels in as I did, arguing with Mother Teresa, and then wrestling with her in my sleep, I wake up in a panic. Did I behave badly toward Mother? What does the dream foretell? Am I Jacob wrestling with the angel to gain God's blessing and enter the promised land? And what part of me is disabled in the fight, as the Bible story goes? Please let it not be my ability to take care of the baby, should mother decide in our favor. Or worse, what if she rejects us entirely? By the time I am dressed to leave the hotel, I have made the decision: whatever Mother comes to in her prayers I can live with. Her decision is out of MY hands.*

~

Today we make sure we reach the Motherhouse as early as 6:00 a.m. We find the back stairway to her office. Sister Frederick, watching the girls scrubbing the floors below, turns toward us with a peace in her face that reassures me I can endure whatever the decision. With such compassion in her voice, she asks us if Mother knows we're here.

"Yes, we've come for an appointment."

"Please be seated." She gestures to a bench across from the

doorway to Mother's office. Here beside me on the bench, Cliff closes his eyes and bows his head in prayer, so unlike him. And then here she is with us again, Mother handing us her formal letter to Margaret Mary to help us get the baby. I don't remember much else, except the way she bent down with folded hands to bless us and to tell us to "bring her up in the fear of God." Again, she was so unhurried with us, so real a person, like someone I had known all my life. I do remember that she came out of her office toward us in her bare feet. I could not help noticing her sore-looking hammer toes. My heart sank to think how she must be suffering, how painful it must be for her just to put one foot in front of the other.

We bow and fold our hands in thanks as prayerfully as we know how and then stumble down the steps. We stop long enough at the bottom to hold each other tight. Then we go to Sister Margaret Mary's office—for more waiting. I don't want to face her "no" again. But after forever she finally appears, makes a big production of gathering us in her arms, and says how she couldn't sleep in the night for having to say no to us, that it would take a *miracle* for us to have that baby. Now she is giving us the papers, still some hesitation when she recalls we are not Catholic and one of us divorced and American on top of all those damned requirements. All I can say to pacify her, to think to say, is yes, but we will give her all our love.

"This we have no doubt of," she finishes her audience with us in her customary authoritative voice without even the suggestion of a smile. We are dispatched with the precious papers and our promise that we will tell no one where the baby came from. We certainly would not want to adversely affect the important work of the Missionaries of Charity, now would we? I remember silently chiding myself for my lack of trust in this holy woman. Could my thoughts be interpreted as sacrilegious?

~

At this stage in the adoption process having received Mother's official approval, we had given ourselves permission to call our daughter Pema, even though we had been talking about Pema or more affectionately Pema-la since we first saw her. All the agency documents referred to her as "Sneha," the name assigned her and agreed to by the Belgians to whom she more or less had been promised. Even the fact that Sneha meant "love" in Bengali could not improve the sound of it. From the beginning, she was Pema, named for the Pema who helped us find her and for the Dalai Lama's sister. Pema was the Tibetan word for lotus flower, full of symbolism and to my eye the most beautiful of aquatic flowering plants. To Buddhists and Taoists, Sacred Lotus (*Nelumbo nucifera*) symbolizes purity and perfection, a thing of beauty whose roots are bound in mud. Also the lotus is rich in spiritual symbolism as one of only four words in the Om mantra of Buddhist compassion, *padme* or *pame,* and combined with *mani,* it is often translated as the jewel-lotus. I wish I could remember the source of this poem:

> *The dew is on the lotus! Rise, great sun!*
> *And lift my leaf and mix me with the wave.*
> *Om Mani Padme Hum, the sunrise comes!*
> *The dewdrop slips into the shining sea!*

After observing how Pema was living at Tindharia's Shanta Bhavan among 40 other little ones—and not the favorite, although surely the most beautiful, at least to our eyes, with those China-doll features, the dark almond-shaped eyes, curly dark-brown hair, and high rounded, flushed cheeks of a Sikkimese or Nepalese or Tibetan—noting the pretty constant fevers and seeing how she was functioning in an orphanage setting, especially in India where only the boys are favored, we were even more anxious to have her in Bangalore with us. With renewed urgency, I returned to the long list of documents required for the adoption and my battle with the Indian postal service. Passage of these papers to and from the States seemed to be taking forever, especially now that we were telling each other we could have her by Christmas. And there was a tough judge yet to crack in Calcutta, we had been told.

~

I had to convey the good news to my best friend Dorothy in Dubuque. How very right she had been in her prescient hope that perhaps Mother Teresa would find us a baby.

> *17 Grant Road Cross*
> *Bangalore 560 001*
> *20 September 1985*

Dear Dorothy,

Well, incredible news. Cliff and I are about to be parents, adoptive parents—is that what you call them, us? And I am wondering if natural parents have this same feeling of being newborn along with the baby. Now almost 10 months old, she's beautiful, Sikkimese we think, a little China-doll face and chubby doll body, serious not-quite-trusting eyes, and she holds herself up with the dignity and mystery of a tiny mountain kingdom. And I love her in my arms. Cliff is even worse smitten. He's a mess. Right away he wanted to know where in Bangalore we could find a playpen, of all things, so he could have her in his office when he's home. Thinks she's going to be an engineer. I say she's going to be a poet-engineer.

To get to Mother Teresa was like climbing the Himalayas—and she didn't turn us away when we reached the top. But to convince her, we had to go three times to her office almost down on our knees. And she's not at all what the media portray—someone larger than life. She's more like a tiny grandmother with a powerful grip. If I ever doubted the hand of God in my life, I don't anymore. The whole of that experience is a very long story I hope to tell you one day soon, along with the dreams for months leading us there. I think of that old Shaker song, "by turning, turning, we come 'round right." How can I describe it to you, this thing of just following my feelings without too much head-talk, and I've stumbled onto what I really want, maybe have wanted for such a long time, this child to love.

So we are deliriously happy, in ways I had hoped for but never quite believed in. See, I had been struggling so long with the decision I thought I had made. Is a child what I really want and if so, why haven't I conceived before now, given two marriages totaling 15 years. Maybe I am too selfish. How will this affect my writing career? Do I have the patience? Am I too old and settled in my ways? All that head talk, ignoring what my heart was beating for such a long time. I had only to analyze my poems and journal scribbles of the last many months or years. Then when we found Pema-la in Darjeeling and loved her on the spot, every door to her slammed in our faces. So I thought all the signs are telling me "no," and I lapsed into hopeless resignation. But bless my husband, Cliff persisted. Then again signs were saying, "Go back up there and get your heart straight, or just go and see if the

Sisters are taking good care of her." And we found a beautiful baby girl and we held her and fed her and loved her little radiant self and we wanted her again even more desperately. Looking back, do you think the months (about nine!) were necessary for me to get used to the idea of being a mother. Weird, huh? Everything has changed, Dorothy. I knew when I arrived in India that it would be a life-changing place I'd been coming to all my life, but I couldn't have said how. Now I know why the path led here.

So far as I can remember, having this child is about the most important event of MY life, coming to her as late as this and in an odd series of turnings, like I have been working or living with this restless dissatisfaction for so long. Cliff and I have so much love to share, have had for such a long time. But no one could have TOLD me. I had to find Pema. You understand.

Will keep you posted.

Love,

Bonnie

Chapter 16

REVERSAL

Again E. M. Forster's Professor Godbole and his ancient phi-losophy call into question our best-laid plans. Try as we might, there is no way we are going to control our future. We may plot our way down paths or imagine our destiny neatly boxed, but all the planning in the world may come to a full stop in a matter of seconds when our course meets reversal. "Whatever the character of life, or its unexpected events," said the writing on the chapel wall at Tindharia. Finding Pema, that unexpected event, and then the split-second decision to adopt her had completely changed the course of our life and hers, and it is about to change again.

~

As best I could understand from Margaret Mary's lack of instruction, the plan was for me to finish the paperwork while the Sisters would bring Pema down the mountain to Calcutta's Nirmala Shishu Bhawan to finish the adop-tion formalities at the Missionaries of Charity. Meanwhile Cliff's wish for a playpen was granted. My dear friend Marcia found the antiquated hand-me-down along with a baby bed, clothes, and other paraphernalia passed around the foreign community. Even so, the shopping list of items not found in Bangalore kept growing longer in anticipation of the next visit to Singapore. I moved my study furnishings out onto the upstairs landing and began stashing all the baby gear in that room in nursery readiness, thinking what curtains to hang, where to place the crib, what closets and drawers to empty—all little rituals performed to bring her to us sooner.

Then came the end of October and a letter on India's inland letter card—a rare appearance in our mail. It was one of those glorious days for which Bangalore was known as the Garden City. A passing monsoon had left everything greener and the light shining crystal. Cliff was just leaving for the West End Hotel for a gathering of company engineers from the States including his boss. My neighbor Kavery and I had just returned from our walk in Lal Bagh Gardens having made a point of strolling the boulevards arcaded with the Gulhomar Tree, Flame of the Forest, its flamboyant blossoms freshly bursting into flame over our heads. I was upstairs puttering in the nursery when our watchman Balraj announced receipt of the mail.

"You will want to see this, Sahib," he said, as if he could read through the thin blue paper. I noticed Cliff's hand shaking when he reached for the letter. In summary, Sr. Margaret Mary had written that Mother Teresa had changed her mind. It was decided in their consciences that we were "not fit" to be the baby Sneha's parents. My first thought was that Mother Teresa does not "change her mind." My next thought was that the paperwork was taking me too long. It was my fault. I was not working fast enough to move the paperwork where it needed to go, tons of it, straight to the target places without all the circumlocutions India practices so well. My third thought, confirmed later by one of Cliff's Catholic colleagues, was that the letter must be yet another test.

"Yep, looks like she's testing you." His wife, who was traveling with him to the company gathering, agreed. She had some experience with Catholic Charities in the states and seemed to know the signs.

"She's testing your sincerity," she prompted. At that, I wanted to raise a mighty protest but thought better of it when I took a good look at Cliff. Since his last trip to Singrauli coal fields, he had been complaining about feeling poorly physically, apart from his immediate reaction to the bad news. He confessed to feeling feverish and head-achy, and his stomach was out of whack, but that wasn't all that unusual in India.

"Surely, it will pass, Cliff," I said. "This is not the time to be sick. We need to stop everything and book a flight to Calcutta now. She listened to our hearts before. She will listen again." No amount of pleading, nothing I said could rouse him, and I could not leave him feeling the way he did.

"I really feel like crap. This has got to be God testing me." Later that day, he could not stand up at the factory and had to call Muthuswamy to come and fetch him home. He stayed in bed for the next 10 days with a fever while the company delegations came and left. Eventually, he thought he needed to risk seeing an Indian doctor. Kavery arranged to have her doctor meet us at the Baptist Hospital. Since it was Muthuswamy's day off, Cliff had to drive the jeep to the hospital himself. Just within sight of the hospital, however, he had to pull over in the shade of a banyan tree to get some relief from the day's heat.

The doctor wanted to know where Cliff's work had taken

him. Had he recently visited an area with open sewers? He told her his itinerary. She confirmed a nasty case of typhoid and proceeded to admit him to the hospital. On the way to his room, we were commenting on how spotlessly clean the place looked. Then midway down the hall we were stopped by a huge cloud issuing from the hospital kitchen. It was the day's chilies under a grease fire. After we were all reduced to coughing fits, Cliff said he felt better already. And when he saw the 1930's hospital room outfitted with a white enamel bed left over from the days of the Raj, he said he was feeling even better.

"I think those chilies really worked the cure," he told the doctor. To me, under his breath, "If I have to die, I'd rather die at home." We collected his prescription at the hospital pharmacy and he turned the jeep back toward Grant Road. We would not be traveling to Calcutta until the antibiotics did their work. Instead, I wrote to Margaret Mary pleading our case once again.

My first letter was full of bitterness and recrimination: I accused the M.C. of being the hand of God that gives and then takes away. It seemed to me that rules had to be followed even in matters of the most heartfelt love. Politics will sully even the most sacred of institutions. My friend Marcia advised me to start over with a new letter.

I knew that Mother had met with us personally and given her permission to us, and on that assurance I based the most imploring love letter of my life. I had changed; India had changed me. I was aware that for the first time in my life, privileged American that I was, I was begging for the only one who would fulfill my life, and she was not "rightfully" mine. I had been found wanting through my stumbling journey to Pema, one step forward and three back. It occurred to me in that writing that I might have reached something like the awareness of Adela Quested at the end of *A Passage to India*: "…she was no longer examining life, but being examined by it; she had become a real person."

REVERSAL

This is the house
on Grant at the cross
that watched the watchman
when he slept,
that held the man
who banged his fist,
that held the woman
when she wept,
that listened for the milk
and hoped for the child.

This is the house
on the palm-studded street
where the daylight climbs
an empty scale of stairs,
where the stone walls sleep
with a flute song
the house might remember.

Chapter 17

LONG DISTANCE CALLING GOD

I *am not sure how I am able to get through the days that follow the letter from Mother or whomever might have sent it. I suspect it is wholly the work of Margaret Mary. Being religious women of the highest order, why in their good consciences do they insist on keeping Pema from us?*

~

Truth to tell, I was having the greatest difficulty finding God in this place, the God of church spires, temperate climes, and my sweet, sheltered childhood. I was feeling sympathy for the Mrs. Moore character in *A Passage*: "…(God) had been constantly in her thoughts since she entered India, though oddly enough he satisfied her less. She must needs pronounce his name frequently, as the greatest she knew, yet she had never found it less efficacious. Outside the arch there seemed always an arch, beyond the remotest echo a silence." On my morning walks through Cubbon Park reserved for prayer, those vast floral, tree-lined arches were empty of the Presence I was accustomed to hearing. I was no longer able to ignore the unkempt state of the park, the organic litter that attracted all manner of bird, insect, and vermin, the holy men squatting and lifting their white dhotis ever so discreetly along the wayside.

Also I could not wrap my imagination around all the resident Hindu gods and goddesses, 30 million of them: the three most important, Brahma the creator, Vishnu the preserver, and Siva the destroyer, but all parts of one GOD. I was trying to fit them into the Biblical trinity, but Brahma had four heads and four arms and rode on Hamsa the goose. Goddess of wisdom Sarasvati was at his side. Vishnu rode the mythical sunbird Garuda with Lakshmi, goddess of wealth. Siva rode Nandi the bull, and Paravati was his consort. Their most popular offspring was elephant-headed Ganesha, god of learning and wisdom, who was mounted on a rat. None of them rode on a donkey.

Recently, even the nasal call to worship of the muezzin was somehow disturbing. The sound of it felt alien, coming so early in the morning from a mosque tower nearby, nothing at all like church bells, or hymns from an organ, or Gregorian chant. The brain fever bird was at it again. All day and into each moonlit night, she repeated her doleful tune—"brain fever, brain-fever." One neighbor explained that she was summoning her lover. In Hindi the call was transcribed *pee-kahan*, meaning "Where is my love?" But the truth is this amorous bird creates her love bower on the twigs borrowed or stolen from babblers, this one in the tall cedar next door competing with the sounds issuing from the minaret.

Cliff, on the other hand, found the Muslim call to prayer soothing. Our differences were growing more pronounced, now that all we had to share was our disappointment. We used to joke about going on separate vacations together. I would comment on the friendly desk clerk in the lobby and the fresh roses. He would complain about the poor service and the rude waiter at breakfast. Without a doubt, he was having a very different experience of India than I was due to the myriad frustrations in his work and travel. For one, he was a lot more susceptible to diseases because of all the unhealthy places he had to visit as his company's sole representative responsible for the entire subcontinent. Language communication was limited. He was studying Hindi, but that was only one of the 24 major languages spoken in India, not to mention more than 100 minor ones. Overnight accommodations were often intolerable, workers were without tools or sufficient knowledge, and tedious formalities and caste-consciousness often slowed the work to a standstill when no one wanted to get their hands dirty on the complex machinery.

Was it fear for Cliff's safety, this feeling that we were definitely not being shepherded "through the valley of the shadow of death?" How many times now had Cliff been hassled at airports, train stations, or on the road at checkpoints going to work-sites mostly in the north? When he first relayed these experiences, he was sort of breezy about them. In Tamil Nadu, for example, he was arrested and taken to jail. They thought he was a spy. He was caught taking pictures near a Tamil Tiger training camp where Palestinians and Libyans were training Sri Lankan Tamils for the Indian-sponsored civil war in Sri Lanka. He said the low-slung jail was like a scene out of a Mexican western circa 1850, complete with a string of jail cells along one side of the hallway and shackles attached to the wall. Happily, Muthuswamy saved the day— Muthuswamy, Cliff's trusty driver, ex-Subedar Major of the Madras Sappers, a demolition team with the engineering division. Before they could shackle Cliff, Muthuswamy pulled out his army ID booklet with his photo in full military dress shiny with medals and everyone jumped to attention. Cliff's driver was a war hero, who had fought in Pakistan twice and China once. And he had the battle scars on the left side of his face to show it. Until his recent retirement, Muthuswamy had been serving as head of engineering at the military's truck driving school. BEML's Colonel Sawhney recommended that Cliff hire him as his driver.

Then another time in Bihar, Cliff's plane was forced to land and everyone evacuated in order to take on a member of parliament with his entourage. For some reason, Cliff was made to board last. He suspected that the Bihar state police, who took care of airport security in a closed room, wanted the contents of his briefcase—things like his retractable pencils and pens that did not leak, his Walkman, his collection of small tools, and his money. However official in their khaki uniforms they looked, these police were at heart thieves. They forced him to open the briefcase and when Cliff was satisfied that they had inspected it sufficiently, he locked it back up. That's when they got rough, pushing Cliff around, shoving him against the wall with their gun butts as Cliff clung to his locked briefcase. Out of nowhere, the Indian Airlines station chief appeared waving the flight manifest and trying to read Cliff's name through smudged glasses.

"Mr. Richeson, Mr. Clifford Richeson," he was yelling with great agitation. Of course he was focused on Cliff since he was the only one left in the airport who fit the description of the foreign name. Cliff's name was on the flight manifest and the plane could not leave without the last passenger. With authority on his side, the pint-sized station chief berated the police for holding up the plane and hustled Cliff to the airport apron. As if Cliff had never for an instant been in harm's way, the flight engineer on the 737 bowed and graciously invited Cliff to take his seat.

Political riots were common enough in Cliff's travels, but the riot he encountered in Bilaspur in a traffic tie-up was the worst, although it was many years afterward that I heard the full details of it. He actually witnessed a murder he was powerless to do anything about. Evidently the wrong political signs on a Leyland truck drew a crowd that started throwing stones. The driver was hit in the forehead full-on with a rock the size of a softball through the windscreen. When he fell out of the truck, they crushed his head with another rock. Then they dragged the young sweeper out of the front seat, broke his arm and beat him up. Meanwhile two local police stood by at some distance leaning on their Enfield Rifles chained to their belts. If the guns had been accessible to Cliff, he said he would have grabbed one and shot the ring-leader. All those years in India, Cliff never let me see the knife he carried in an ankle sheath made out of an Ace bandage.

There should have been nothing to fear, however, here at home in Bangalore. The company insisted we have 24-hour watchman service. We were surrounded by neighbors of all stripes, native Hindu and Muslim, both Tamil and Kana-da-speaking, retired Church of England. We counted them all true friends who would look out for us. I had Cliff's driver Muthuswamy, an armed war hero accompanying me wher-ever I went, whenever I stepped out of the Ambassador, that tank-like relic of the British Empire. But what about that time I had strayed from my beaten path and been chased by women brandishing cow-piles and taunted by children who should have been in school? Everyone cautioned us to be on guard against attacks by the "armies of beggars." Kavery said it was a sad state of affairs, India's blatant poverty and lack of education.

~

To keep our distances, Cliff was finding more reasons to be off on his motorcycle, while I stared at the typewriter or walked Cubbon Park alone. There I carried all my prayers and my promises. I was not a hardened smoker or drinker, but I promised God that if I were so blessed, I would welcome this baby totally free of all my bad habits that might conceivably harm her. I would cultivate more patience where the needs of my husband were concerned. I would carry on with the Quakers even though I was not comfortable hosting the Meeting for Worship any longer. It had moved elsewhere. To sit in silence was to sit in agonizing impatience, when I could be doing something to further the only cause that mattered—getting Pema. Waiting in silence for divine inspiration in the Quaker way felt like an exercise in frustration. I was deaf to it. I could not find the peace inside myself, much less advocate for the wider one. I felt like a sham.

The lure to Cubbon Park now was a small Hindu fertility shrine just on the edge of the Park I had never had the courage to visit. Maybe I was hedging my bets. It is hard to say now what was motivating my fascination for the shrine. I took a new route, broke off from the main artery and cut across a ragged field so as to approach the temple in a wide sweep from behind and unobserved. The footpaths were interrupted by two evil-looking stone wells, enormous circles about 20 feet in diameter once covered with granite slabs, now partly open to the murky pools far below. Each time

I passed, a nameless something compelled me to chance a look over the edge. It must have been the same impulse that over-rode my mother's constant caution never to look in a broken mirror.

I took my chances against seven years bad luck and peered over the brink into the darkness thinking there might be something afloat worth rescuing—like an ill-fated bride. Now that bride-burning had almost run its course in India, so they said, the well had become a popular form of dispensing with a woman once all the available dowry had been bled from her family. Too frequently, the newspapers reported these instances of fatal abuse in a small square of print or a Sunday magazine feature, rank with gruesome details. I had yet to discover an unwanted bride in one of these pits. All the same something always crept across my scalp here.

My circuitous path crossed more scorched stubble and a line of bedraggled eucalyptus poles until the dusty sky closed over a woody shade, leafy thickets of bamboo and the wide-spreading *gulmohar* that provided a good cover. In my disguise, I busied myself collecting seeds, flowers, all sorts of plant specimens that reached home only to accumulate in a dry pile.

In the distance, I saw an ancient *peepul* or *bodhi* tree (*Ficus religiosa*) forming a centerpiece, growing like a giant mushroom out of the raised platform of the shrine. I could never resist picking up at least one leaf from the litter on the ground around a *bodhi* tree. What was it about this leaf that was so appealing? Perhaps the perfect shape, a broadly oval fan strong in the spine that suddenly narrowed at the apex into a long tip, and depending on which way you turned it, you saw a long-nosed spade or a heart with string attached to nothing. Shiny and flat, the leaves hung pendulous so that even a slight breeze set them shimmering.

The Thais and Burmese had the right idea, fashioning their temple bells with clappers in the shape of these sacred fig leaves so as to move with the wind. Even in the hand, the leaf's still form somehow kept generating life. Of course, I thought of the Buddha lore attached to the *bodhi* tree. It was under such a spreading fig as this that the Gautama Buddha was said to sit in meditation for so long at Bodh-Gaya and eventually to receive enlightenment. And there were tales some substantiate as fact that a certain specimen in old Ceylon lived well over 2000 years and was reported still thriving. Orthodox Hindus will never cut down a *bodhi* tree but generously cultivate them for the blessings they bring, never mind that they strangle whatever may grow in their path.

Stone pedestals supported miniature monoliths of entwining snakes covering the shrine, a host of what appeared to be blackened stone dolls known as "the planets," and the jovial image of round-bellied Ganesha, seated on his haunches. This was the elephant god whose special province was every new enterprise. One hut enclosed the knobby lingam, a stylized phallus, surrounded by the yoni, a stylized vagina. Those petitioning for offspring, preferably male heirs, would do *pujah* with a coconut broken over the fertility stone so that the sweet water flowed down the yoni canal. But Naga, the snake god, not the fearsome creature of the west but a protective force, dominated the scene. In rows like crude tombstones, cobras were carved in relief in every configuration, draped with garlands of fresh marigolds and smudged with a red dust.

A bell sounded and I remembered why I had come. A

long-haired priest in western shirt and short-tailed dhoti began his rounds. Soon the religious complex was alive with flickering flames and the fragrance of burning incense. From the looks of the humble clientele, I knew that this was no rich man's temple where the holy family was protected behind bars and a collection box. It was an open, all-purpose place of worship serving every sort of need, although the priest informed me with a glare that tourists were not welcome.

Women and dusty-haired children had settled on the steps that mounted to a pink stupa capped by a bright orange lotus bud. I could only imagine that this was the meeting place for their morning gossip. Hungry-looking dogs with their ribs showing through furless patches cowered on the perimeter. Way overhead from one of the topmost bodhi branches came the pariah kite whistle, a delicate trill too small for the size and appetite of this bird.

At times I was distracted in my pilgrimage by a beggar clutching at my sleeve or an old crone on the shrine steps, the ragged end of her sari covering her gray head like a kerchief.

"Maaa…Maaa," she called, her hands folded in the customary respectful greeting, lightened by a laugh and a wave. She was beckoning me to shed my walking staff and my shoes, to enter her world of twisted snakes and burnt icons and mute cosmic forces that somehow kept functioning after 5,000 years in the lives of so many millions of Indians.

So I dropped my staff in the freshly swept dirt path, folded my hands and bowed my head to the old woman, to the *bodhi* tree, to the incredibly complex wonder of it all. And then I fell on my knees and sobbed to the only God I knew, praying for the baby girl I wanted and could not have.

THE BEGGARS' CARNIVAL

See the armless-legless man
wheeled out in wondrous disguise
like an old lawnmower.
You must never meet his eyes
or you'll empty your pockets
in the dung-filled street
and he'll be laughing rupees
up his empty sleeves.
See the twisty-limbed boy
like a crab gone wrong
pinching unsuspecting tourists
by the seaside ruins.
Hear the children hordes
in Fury pursuit
chant, "Ma, Ma, Maaaaaa"
like dolls on the squeeze
and the silent ones
collapsed on the curb
for sleep or for dead
like wounded birds
or sacked like potatoes
by a mute tin cup.
See the hunchback and tongueless,
the lame and the leprous,
the dark pencil stubs
that stab at your skirt.
And the wise will tell you

they're tricksters and thieves
and if you're not wary
they'll steal more than your sleep,
for this is the way
the beggars play
on the streets of holy India
all day.

Part III
TOO MUCH TO HOPE

Chapter 18

ALMOST OURS

In mid-November, at approximately the one-year-old mark of Pema's birth, or when we calculated her birth, another letter on India's thin blue inland stationery arrived. This time the hand-written letter came from a Sister Damien summoning us to the Motherhouse in Calcutta. I cabled Cliff in Nagpur to meet me at the Oberoi Grand in Calcutta at the same time that he was trying to cable me to meet him there. He had just been called to Calcutta to attend a conference sponsored by Detroit Diesel and had decided to try for an audience with Mother Teresa one more time. The cables crossed in passage. Cliff knew nothing about the letter from Sister Damien. I knew nothing about his planned attempt to see Mother Teresa. We might have checked in separately, gone to our separate rooms since it was very late, and never seen each other except for our chance meeting in the lobby.

"Wait a minute," he said, holding me at arm's length as if I were an apparition. "How can this be? I just cabled you this morning. If I didn't know better, I would say this was another Dionysia-inspired mysterious encounter! She's trying to teach us to believe in miracles!"

"Obviously you did not receive my cable! I wonder if this means we may have been given a reprieve." And I handed him Sr. Damien's letter.

~

Next morning, I could not wait for Cliff to finish his Coal India meeting. I went to Shishu Bhavan, the Calcutta orphanage just a few blocks from the Motherhouse, hoping to see Pema there, praying that the Belgians had not already come for her. I found her among other children in a play area with a viewing section of child-sized chairs reserved for adults. I did not dare go to her for fear that I wasn't allowed to touch her. I simply watched, her little diapered bottom uppermost in the air, as she crawled with determination toward a pile of toys and one in particular. It was one of those modern activity boards with knobs and buttons to push and pull to produce noises or pop outs. She was clearly interested and engaged while the other children just sat there showing no curiosity whatsoever. I had to control my need to get down there on all fours with her.

Later that day Cliff and I met with Sister Damien, who had replaced Sister Margaret Mary as head of adoptions. After prayerful consideration, Mother's organization had decided to shift Pema to the Society for International Child Welfare (S.I.C.W.) known as "sea-cue," since they were "better qualified" to work with American families, she said. Pema would be well taken care of there, on the other side of Calcutta, while the paperwork was finishing. In truth, I had to ask myself what took M.C. so long to give up Pema to an adoption agency that was accustomed to dealing with Americans, as M.C. clearly was not!

As usual, the phones were uncooperative, or we had the wrong number. We finally were able to reach Nina Nayak, Secretary of the Society at S.I.C.W. and went in the late morning to iron out the details of the transfer. We returned to Shishu Bhavan for a warm and sleepy time with Pema, who refused to look at me until we were leaving and it was almost dark. She did accept the rag-doll Jane had sent her but with not a whole lot of interest. All I wanted to do was hold her and hold her.

I could tell she had grown in the two months since last seeing her at Tindharia, even more round and beautiful, a shy, serious little thing, probably wondering about this strange white woman who kept turning up at odd moments. She had been at Calcutta since 28 October and seemed confident with the staff.

Next day I went to the American Consulate to meet with our favorite Consul Mr. McCall. I needed reassurance that we were working in an orderly and timely way. Then I collected Cliff after his meeting and we spent the rest of the morning with Pema in the orphanage dining hall with other hopeful parents. We chatted with an Indian couple waiting to adopt a one-month-old boy. The wife was wearing what looked to be her best gold-trimmed saree. A large red tikka adorned her forehead.

"You must be pleased," she said. "The baby is so relaxed with you. You will be good parents."

"And in only a day or two you will be the ones feeding her," said the dear old Bengali amah who was spooning rice porridge into Pema. If only she were right! And I remember the briefest conversation with the white-haired grandma from Switzerland whose mission had been to deliver medicines for diarrhea. She smiled and chatted prayerfully with us while fingering the rosary around her neck.

Pema reached for the camera with the same curiosity she had reached for the toys yesterday. Her tiny fingers grasped it and kept patting it as if it were something really special. Then I remembered about the rag-doll Jane sent. Oh well, that hardly seemed worth pursuing. It would probably go the way of all the orphanage toys, in a heap for sharing. We had what we wanted, or thought we did.

My thoughts aimed all toward readiness, all that I had to do in the weeks ahead, the rest of the paperwork, the home study, the strength to take on the weight of motherhood at age 42. Was it Sarah in the *Old Testament*, so old she was and still fertile? Just give me that baby, I prayed, to show what a woman can do with love and faith. Undoubtedly behind my strong faith was Cliff, loving Pema as I did. I loved the way he loved her, tended her, wanted to hold her and find joy in her just as I did. They were so peaceful with each other that she fell asleep on his lap. I thanked God for his bursting heart, for the sweet look of tenderness that lit up his father's face, the father I never had. How could I be so lucky, so blessed?

~

I had not dared to ask about Margaret Mary. A year's experience had taught me that she was not to be trusted. Call it superstition, but there was still the fear that she had the power to reverse our luck again. Still I wondered what might have happened to her. I wanted to but then thought better of asking Sr. Damien about her as we were on our way out of the office. She and Cliff were still in conversation when I stepped out into the driveway and caught my breath. There was my nemesis sitting in the back seat of a parked Ambassador wearing a neck brace. My first un-gracious thought was "Serves her right!"

When I leaned down to take her hand, Margaret Mary reached up and pinched my cheek as if I were a naughty schoolgirl, once lost but now returned to the fold. When I asked how she was, she answered that she was being transferred to New Delhi.

"Did you receive my letter?" she asked.

"No, only the letter from Sr. Damien."

"Now you have what you want," she said, as if somehow she had lost the battle and I had won. "Maybe she will bring you to God. Just make sure you do not spoil that baby!" And she motioned the driver to move on. I smiled, extended my hand in a polite wave, and thought that if it were not for the sanctity of this place that humbled me so and my Quaker sensibility that always counseled peace, I would tell her how self-righteous she was and that she had no right to stand in judgment over my faith! I did enjoy the look of horror I imagined on her face if she should see the stash of Christmas packages that were mounting high as the Himalayas in the nursery upstairs in Bangalore. It went without saying, however, that we would not have our daughter in time for Christmas.

The letter Margaret Mary asked about referred to Pema's transfer to S.I.C.W. with mention of our social worker in Bangalore, Sarina. Evidently, all along Sarina had been working diligently behind the scenes to negotiate Pema's transfer. I wondered how many more "tests" we would have to pass before we actually had Pema in our arms forever.

~

By January 20, all the papers for adoption had arrived, been carefully gathered and couriered up to Calcutta, stamped and sealed red, gold, and purple enough to impress any bewigged judge. I was waiting to hear if more papers or revisions were needed before I returned to Calcutta to thrust myself on Pema and smother her with all this pent-up mother's love. Also I had supplies for Sister Damien—pens (I gathered fist-fulls), an alarm clock, sturdy toys, and useful what-nots. The Calcutta agency S.I.C.W. had sent two photos taken of Pema around mid-December. She was standing firm as a Buddha on all twos in one photo and stretching long, less chubby-looking legs in the other photo, actually throwing a tantrum I think in that one—something like both sides of the coin in the message?

I had also hired a full-time cook and cleaning ayah, tiny aged "ma" but very experienced after three years working for German families. She arrived at each daybreak armed with a woven bag about half her size and filled with untold necessities. Already she had the respect of the rest of the staff and had devised methods of getting at things even I could not reach. She expected no interference from me. I loved it, feeling the weight of Atlas lifted. I firmly believed Heaven had sent Margret to help me move the next Mt. Kanchenjunga. The significance of her name was not lost on me. She was here to undo the damage Margaret Mary had tried to do. And Cliff was happy as a lamb with regular meals guilt free.

So lovely to have TIME to actually write in the mornings, to wait quiet, patient as a bird blending into branch and foliage. Damn it. I've got this place working for me now, just like Singapore finally, and we're moving again soon. I haven't nearly finished with India. If I spent the rest of my life here, I'd probably say the same—in my dotage, a tired, shriveled-up old woman stretched out on a rope cot, a wad of betel bulging my jaw and jasmine garlands fixed in a sparse gray bun, waiting for Margret's daughter to bring me a bowl of rice, a bucket of hot water or for a Sai Baba to transport me to Nirvana. How can I leave India knowing so little about her? This strange attachment I can't yet account for, except that she continues to mystify me. How does a land so difficult of living, so full of complexity, be at the same time so welcoming?

~

The last of the many getting-Pema-letters I penned was written to my old friend Donna Page, an artist living and working in New York as a restorer of African art objects. She, a single mom, was preparing to adopt a little girl.

But first, my cable to Cliff:

CLIFF RICHESON
C/O UNIVERSAL GLAMOUR TRADING CO.
TAIPAI
11987 UNIGLACO
PEMA DOWN WITH CHICKEN POX IN QUARAN-
TINE UNTIL MARCH 14!SHALL I AWAIT YOUR
ARRIVAL BANGALORE MID-MARCH OR GO UP
WITHOUT YOU? MY WISH THAT YOU JOIN ME
FOR "DELIVERY" IN CALCUTTA UPON RETURN
FROM H K.CAN? LOVE. BT
RIGHT NOW PLAN TO FLY UP AROUND 10
MARCH. WILL LEAVE WHEREABOUTS WITH
BEML, CALCUTTA AND KAVERY.

17 Grant Road Cross
Bangalore 560 001
India
27 February 1986

Dear Dona-Dona,

I think I must have led you astray. No, we don't have Pema even now, after so many frustrating months when she is near yet so far away. As of mid-February, we learned that the Calcutta High Court had given us guardianship, and last week I was all set to go up there to take motherly possession. Then last Saturday a telegram arrived announcing she has the chicken pox! and would be in quarantine for 3 weeks, or until mid-March. So more interminable waiting when I just want to get on with our future together.

Back to the typewriter and now a more expensive courier service rather than the unpredictable bullock-drawn express that is the Indian postal service. Of course everything, home-study locally and all the documents you know about, had to pass through the Illinois agency plus the Dept. of Children and Family Services, Springfield, plus U.S. Immigration and Naturalization, which goes on and on, even now. When I go up to get her in Calcutta, I must check in with the American Consulate for more paperwork there. Luckily, they're used to these procedures. But I'm feeling a real sense of accomplishment in the fact that all those documents actually passed through the Calcutta High Court, in spite of regular changes in the law and impossible bureaucracy. In truth, I suspect that both known and unknown forces were working behind the scenes, have been at work all along, on our behalf, both here and stateside. Sr. Dionysia, the nun who was most supportive throughout those many months, confessed to us that she had discreetly tucked Pema away whenever interested potentially adoptive parents came to visit at Tindharia.

As you probably guessed, Mother's (my mother, Hawthorne's) reaction was much like yours at the outset. Too much responsibility at too advanced an age. That was in the early months. Once she understood from long explanatory letters that I was absolutely serious and in love with this child, then she backed off gradually and now she is sending letters full of encouragement mixed with her mother's worry. The last one said, "As soon as you get Pema, don't let her out of your sight." I'm not sure what prompted that piece of warning, as if I don't have my own set of anxieties. Mainly I'm wondering how Pema will take to me/us now at this new independent age of 16 months. Will she come willingly or put up a dramatic fuss. So I'm planning to spend as much time as possible with her before we launch her on the airplane. And Cliff is in Taiwan. I've wired him to meet me in Calcutta but wonder if he'll receive the message. Will I be able to handle Pema thru the turmoil of Calcutta airport on my own? Once she's here, I feel as though I can manage because everything awaits her comfort and easy exploration, lots of toys and a very welcoming, loving environment. I'm full of fears, little and big; I suppose that's normal enough. Overriding these is this great love in my heart I want to share with Pema. I try not to have expectations for her. Just want her to be her own little person growing into a big person with us. I suspect she'll have a lot to teach me. Something tells me she's a very old soul.

Please write soon and tell us your news about the upcoming show, the book, and what's happening with your ADOPTION.
Love,
Bonnie

PEMA'S SONG IN THE KEY OF D

They won't believe you
When they see you.
They won't believe their eyes.
I try to tell them in letters
But, I can't describe you…
…Are a darling,
There's no denying.
You're indescribable.
They won't believe you
When they see you.
No, they won't believe their eyes.

Chapter 19

ANNOUNCEMENT

F inally the day arrived in March—March 11, 1986 to be exact—when we were allowed to fetch Pema from S.I.C.W. Although she had recovered from the chicken pox, she retained a little fever which made her somewhat listless. While Cliff was tending to the final paperwork, I carried her in my arms to the mini-zoo constructed just across the street outside the front door of the orphanage. An odd assortment of animals, mostly pigeons and rabbits, were stacked in cages one on top of the other behind wire mesh. I tried making up stories about the animals, giving them names, but the fever or the medication used to treat it diminished any interest she might have had. Also I wasn't sure how much of my English she understood, since the language spoken by the nuns and the workers in all the orphanages was mainly Bengali.

Next day, while Cliff was finishing the paperwork at the hotel, Pema and I took a taxi to the airport. There we sat together, Pema nestled in my lap, a little overheated, trying not to go to sleep. I had a set of nesting cups in my carry-on which she made quick work of and then lost interest. The flight delay seemed long. I was eager to get her to her new

Pema and Bonnie at the menagerie facing S.I.C.W., Calcutta

home and all the toys to explore waiting there. Mainly I was
nervous about what I would do if someone thought to question me about my right to have her in my possession. And
there was no sign yet of Cliff. Might not someone either in
the crowd or behind a desk accuse me of child theft? In order
to get her to Bangalore as soon as possible, we had decided
to forego waiting for her passport. I wasn't sure just how
convincing my S.I.C.W. paperwork would be to an inquisitive
official who might notice the difference between the child
with dark brown features and the dirty-blond, green-eyed
mother. Cliff managed to turn up just as I had to present our
tickets. Pema was dozing with her head buried in my shoulder.
We made it on the plane without the anticipated struggle.
Then and there, I vowed I would dye my hair dark brown.

Would it ever feel like Pema belonged to me? For more
years than I can say, there was never a ride on an airplane, a
ferry, a train, or any form of transportation requiring us to

show our citizenship papers that I did not hold her tight in my arms and look smiling defiance into the eyes of anyone in authority who I feared might take her away from me.

~

Cliff took it upon himself to write our parents about the final stages of Pema's adoption. He knew how anxious they were to know every detail.

17 Grant Road Cross
Bangalore 560 001
India
March 1986

Dear Mom and Dad and Hawthorne,

I know you are all excited to hear about the baby so I want to get this on the way quickly. Photos will follow soon, probably next week.

I got back from Hong Kong on 8 March; Bonnie and I flew to Calcutta on 10 March; and we left Calcutta with Pema on 12 March. We had planned to wait in Calcutta until her passport came through but as soon as we saw her we knew we wanted her home with us, and no one could tell us how long the wait would be. They will send her passport by courier.

Pema took to the air with no fuss. She loves to travel. She likes places with lots of activity. Everybody on our staff loves her. Our ayah Margret just adores her and plays with her. Her favorite thing is to sit on a stool looking out the back door where the cats are. Today she was watching the dhobi (laundryman) iron our clothes in the carport and the watchman fix up her borrowed wicker high chair. She loves people and animals. The back screen door serves as her TV. She sits there contentedly watching her new world go by.

She just got over the chickenpox and still has marks all over her little body. She has a bit of a cold. The first morning she was here Bonnie took her to the Baptist Hospital to see the doctor. He won her heart and she his. We now have a pediatrician. He says she is in good shape except for the cold and scabies which he is treating. We will take her to our doctor in Singapore. Dr. Waddell will be delighted to see her. He does pediatrics, too. The Scotsman came to the East with the British forces as medical officer with the Ghurkas during the Emergency in Malaysia. Most of the Ghurkas come from a place not far from Darjeeling called Kurseong. He feels like we do about the mountain people.

There has been a long line of visitors to see Pema. After seeing her, they understand why we fought so long to get her. She is without a doubt the most beautiful child for many a mile. The pictures don't do her justice. She has some of the cutest expressions you have ever seen. Loveable or not, between her and the visitors we are worn out. The first morning she was up twice, once at about 3:00 a.m. and again at 4:45 a.m. I think she was being Muslim and answering the morning call to prayer. Today she got up at 5:30 a.m. That is more like Buddhist prayer time. Maybe if we are lucky she will think she is a Catholic and not get up until 10 o'clock Mass tomorrow. Her morning nap was disturbed by visitors and she refused her afternoon nap. Bonnie finally lay down while Margret tried to get Pema to sleep. She wouldn't have anything to do with me at the time. Bonnie took her for a walk in the backpack carrier. She liked that so well I took her for a walk, too. She loves to be outside, especially where there is lots of activity, people, traffic or animals. Neither animals nor loud noises frighten her. She likes music, especially the tapes of flute music. Dolls and teddy bears don't interest her. Nesting cups, blocks and crayons keep her occupied. She doesn't draw with the crayons.

She tucks them under her arm. That is how they used to take her temperature with a thermometer at the orphanage, we learned.

She can stand alone and walk with help. She walks for Margret but not for me. Margret has a strong physical resemblance to her favorite ayah at the orphanage, so she took to her quickly. But it is clear to her who her mother is. Guests will come and want to hold her, but she always reaches for Bonnie. She talks to herself and I think she has the beginnings of a couple of words. She said "apah" this afternoon. She didn't say it to anyone. She just babbled along to herself. She lets me feed her, even today when she wouldn't have anything else to do with me. I make her cereal and milk and feed her. Diapers are Bonnie's department. In computer terms, you could say I handle the input and Bonnie gets the output. We found out neither of us knew how to pin on a diaper. We have it sorted out now, but it took a few trials. Disposable diapers as we know them are not available here. We have to ration the few we brought in from Singapore and Hong Kong. We save them for traveling. Living in Hong Kong will be much easier with all the convenience supplies.

Currently we plan to spend a few days in Singapore to renew our passports around 7 April and then return to India. I will do some work in Taiwan and then we will begin the move about June. We should be on our way to Hong Kong by July. That will be the hot season for them. Our hot season here in the south has just started. It should peak in May. Right now the days are hot and the nights cool. Later on the days get hotter and the nights do not get cool. I was hoping to avoid this, but the work in Taiwan can't wait. It is probably better anyway for Pema to get settled into this home and used to us before we uproot her again and go into another month or two transition period in Hong Kong.

We can't wait to get home with her. We know you are going to love her. She is beautiful and a rugged little trooper. In 16 months she has survived four orphanages and almost half that time in Calcutta. She has been stealing hearts all the way.

I must end this and get to bed. Pema went to sleep at 7:00 p.m. Looks like we'll be up for the morning call to prayer!
Love,
Cliff

On top of Cliff's letter to our parents, we sent a simple postcard to all our friends and family. On the cover was Henry Moore's *Family Group* (1948-49), a bronze casting of mother, father, and child in the collection at the Museum of Modern Art, New York. On the reverse I wrote the following words:

> *She is here.*
> *Pema has come to us at last.*
> *We hold her*
> *light as our breath,*
> *deep in our dreaming,*
> *and pray she will not fly away*
> *before we have loved her enough.*
> > *Bonnie & Cliff*
> > *Bangalore, March 1986*

What to do with a 16-month-old when you have had no experience whatsoever of very young children? Apart from tending to her physical needs—bathing, dressing, feeding, nappy changing, checking for fever, medicating—all of which we could get a handle on fairly quickly with the help of Margret, what to do with the remaining hours in the day? I guess I thought that we would just love her, although I had no clear picture what that might look like on an all-day basis.

Pema in the dining room at home on Grant Road, Bangalore

Out of an uncorked lamp, the genie materializes in a puff of smoke and grants your heart's desire. What happens next?

As soon as the fever passed and Pema was fully alert, the challenge began. It was Margret who came to the rescue, tiny, wiry, bespectacled Margret, blind as a bat. She had come to us fresh from a German family carrying her oversized tote-bag to manage yet another foreign household with an air of take-charge authority. Right away Cliff sent her with Muthuswamy to find an eye doctor and get her proper glasses.

At some point, she looked up at me through those wide-screened lenses in a permanent state of smudge and always askew, as if life had too many demands to deal with glasses. She looked at me as if to say, "You cannot sit there and just look at her, like star-struck new parents." Margret was too well-mannered Indian to say that. Instead, this is how she put it.

"Pema has all these toys. May I suggest you join her on the

floor." She laid down beach towels and pillows on the hard black marble floor, certainly not the best seating for a little one. We had rented the house because it was newly built, no one else had lived in it, and its surrounding stone walls did not have intimidating shards of broken glass embedded on top. That was before any dream of a baby Pema. I decided our next house would be wall-to-wall carpeted.

During these weeks with Margret by my side, cooking and cleaning, sweeping and swabbing, it occurred to me that she meant so much more to me than a cleaning ayah. She was providing the courage and mothering that a new mother needs. Little by little, Margret dispelled my fear of not being "enough mother" by simply giving all to know that I was, that is Pema's mother. She did not want to take over or steal Pema's affection. When the time came to leave Margret, I was feeling much more qualified.

Whether Pema understood me or not, given her history of multi-lingual care-takers, I got pretty good at inventing stories based on an array of stuffed toys, building blocks, nesting cups, and trucks. Those were Cliff's contribution to the play area, just in case she might want to grow up to be an engineer. And there was Thomas the Tank Engine in the form of a push toy meant to encourage her to walk. But she was more interested in climbing the open wood and iron stairs leading to the second floor, another reason to move on to safer surroundings.

My greatest happiness was the daily walk to Cubbon Park. I would tuck Pema inside the sling kiddy-carrier as best I could with her facing me, and we would head for the park swings. I had read the instructions on the package from Mothercare, but they didn't say anything about how both of us were supposed to fit between straps, buckles, and padding. Was there something the manufacturer wasn't telling me, like it was designed for Mia Farrow svelte, or what? Only later did I see an image of what we were supposed to look like. It was meant to be a backpack, but I wanted to be able to see her! So I carried her frontal.

There was so much to delight a child at the Park: birds, squirrels, insects, the long brigades of ants building super-highways to the morning sacrifice of rice and lentils some devotee had placed in the crux of the stilt roots buttressing the old kapok tree. Now that life in Bangalore had returned to its placid self, one day I had the courage even to walk with Pema all the way to Lal Bagh Botanical Gardens and the Bull Temple. Just inside the temple was a huge replica of Nandi the bull draped with jasmine garlands. The Hindu priest invited us to step inside. He left briefly to return with a jasmine garland which he placed around Pema's tiny neck.

I would like to give the impression that I conducted my parenting with model patience, but that would be a lie. During the move from Bangalore to Hong Kong, I received three, count them three, letters from Dorothy with advice on how to deal with "grumpiness." Something I divulged in a letter must have truly worried her. About one month into Pema's homecoming, I remember one incident in particular. It was late at night, and nothing I did could persuade Pema to fall asleep. I was at the end of my rope, sleep-deprived, and weary. I felt I had no choice but to leave the nursery with the night-light on and the door open to the well-lit hallway. Cliff was downstairs in his office trying to finish some paperwork. The noise from upstairs was just another form of agitation on his long list.

Family Group, Henry Moore, 1948-49 MOMA, N.Y.

It was hot. The windows were open and evidently her crying could be heard down Grant Road Cross. Mrs. Mathias, the grandmother from the compound next door, came to see if she could help. I met her at the front door.

"Mrs. Mathias, I know that you mean well, but I believe I can handle this myself." After waiting approximately 15 months, 21 days and 17 hours for the delivery of this baby, I was not about to admit that I was incapable of dealing with any emergency.

Cliff came out of his office to order me upstairs. That was the last straw. We had a shouting match and I finished by turning my back on him and marching into the kitchen. He followed me and then slammed the door that led from the kitchen to the dining room and the rest of the house. A towel hanging on the door knob got stuck in the door and I could not open it. I was trapped inside the kitchen. Meanwhile Pema's hollering took on an even more urgent tone and something told me I had to get to her at once. Had she somehow fallen out of the bed and hurt herself? But how could I get to her? I was locked in the kitchen. I called to the night watchman. There was no response. He was not about to interfere in his employer's domestic issues.

I began banging on the door, the walls, even the window to the back passageway. I was looking for some device sharp and heavy enough to break the window to get out when Cliff finally freed me. It took some effort because the door would not budge. Once freed, I ran upstairs to find Pema standing up and holding for dear life onto the railing of the bed. My heart broke. It occurred to me that her residence with us was the first time in her whole short life that she had been in a room alone. I picked her up and gathered all of her into my arms and just held her until she was quiet. Somehow I knew to do that, to cuddle her and keep cuddling her, even though I had not yet received Dorothy's letters with her loving mother's advice to that effect.

In Dorothy's letter of August 22, 1986 she said, "Jenny had a good snicker when I read your question about if I ever got cross or cranky. Of course I did! One thing I found helpful when either of us was crabby was to pick her up and cuddle. That seemed to calm both of us. However, kids are all different, and I have had other mothers tell me their kids didn't 'cuddle.' I'm not the least bit worried about your being a good mother. You are a warm and loving creature. Just trust your instincts and have a lot of quiet times together. It really is hard sometimes not to feel consumed totally during those early years, but the attention then pays enormous dividends later."

Chapter 20

CITIZENSHIP

"This is full of fiction," Cliff said, examining Pema's passport. "Her eyes and hair are dark brown, not black. Anybody can see that. And 'place of birth' is not Calcutta." What's more, her sweet face was full of fear and about to dissolve in tears. Her thumbprint was a tiny purple blur. Upon closer scrutiny, we discovered that it was not endorsed for travel to Singapore, for the planned week's stop-off celebration in April before our next destination and future home, Hong Kong.

At the last minute, I had to rush to the local passport office, Ministry of External Affairs, Government of India, in downtown Bangalore to see if they could help us. We were scheduled to fly out of Madras in three days. My experience with these government offices did not promise hope. Mr. C. Janakiraman, the Superintendent of Passports, was actually there, although it was Friday and past quitting time, and the entrance to his chamber was barred. By now, getting accustomed to an unfolding pageantry of miracles, I was not surprised to find access to the building as soon as dear Muthuswamy stepped forward and flashed his military retirement card.

The very gracious Superintendent, seated like a judge on his elevated bench, noted that Pema's passport was restricted to the U.S., U.K., Lebanon, the Republic of Egypt, and all countries in Europe, which did not include Singapore. He fully agreed that these restrictions were "a silly thing," and he said he would fix it. Since this would require endorsement from the Calcutta office where the passport had been issued and we were pressed for time, he graciously offered to call Calcutta to see what he could do. Next miracle: the call went through on the first try. With Calcutta's permission given, our savior deleted the earlier endorsement by the name smudged but clearly titled Regional Passport Officer, Calcutta, and replaced it with one valid for travel to all countries except the Republic of South Africa, for some odd reason. I did not argue. His final stamp echoed through the empty government halls. We were free to travel to Singapore to introduce our daughter to long-awaiting friends and our family doctor. The next trip out of India was a little more problematic, of course.

~

Events moved swiftly once we had Pema and knew where we were going. The route to Hong Kong and our new home had to pass through Delhi and all the government paper-work, tax payments, and necessaries to free of us of Indian residency. More importantly, Pema was required to pass a physical examination by a US Immigration-approved doctor before she could leave India. The worry was the set of x-rays we were carrying from the S.I.C.W. Foundling Home that showed shadowy patches on her lungs. These could have been interpreted as signs of TB, still rampant in India and in all the places our daughter had lived.

Again more of the miracle unfolding, the Sikh doctor who examined her had been trained at Parkland Hospital in Dallas, the same hospital made famous by the 1963 assassination of President Kennedy. When the doctor left the room, Cliff was able to read the fine print on his medical license and figured that our doctor had been in residency during that fateful event, which may have explained his sympathy for us. No, he could see no indication whatsoever of TB. The marks were indicative of pneumonia and would eventually go away, but she would have to be treated for giardia as soon as we reached Hong Kong. Both Pema and I had been suffering from giardia for well over a month. Whatever form of Flagyl that had been dispensed to us in Bangalore was not working.

I am sorry to say that I became an expert on giardia, that is, the variety of the infection native to India. This is a water-borne parasite, a protozoa shaped like a tennis racket, that attaches itself to the stomach lining with the idea of dis-couraging any wish you might have to play tennis or lead an active life. It lives best in the water systems around play or nursery schools and public swimming pools. My guess is that it somehow reached the crude chalk-filtered water system in my Bangalore kitchen, although thankfully Cliff never succumbed. Giardia is happiest when you are not. You live in a constant state of lethargy. The only time you feel at all well is just after eating a meal. Then slowly, inexorably, nausea sets in again and then the urge to go to the bathroom and then the inevitable, inexhaustible diarrhea.

All the photos from those weeks show Pema and me look-ing away, dull and distracted, while everyone else around us is animated and grinning ear to ear. At a going-away celebration at the Jamal's home, there is Mushtaq pulling

Jamal family in Bangalore

his sister's hair. Adela is giving him a good shove, while Silu, the dad, is craning his neck anticipating the future pranks of his children. I cannot count the number of cotton nappies soiled with runny yellow goo I hand-washed, since there was nothing like disposable diapers in Bangalore. Come to think of it, we did have a stash sent from Singapore, but I was hoarding them for the time we would need them during the move. I could have kissed the stewardess on the British Airways flight to Hong Kong when she slipped a package of nappies into my lap without a word.

Sure enough, the hotel doc in Hong Kong fixed us up with the medicine we needed. Within a short time, Pema was cured with the regular doses of syrup he prescribed. My case seemed to linger on forever. Searching for a permanent residence in a totally strange foreign city was difficult enough, but I could also boast a working familiarity with every available

public toilet between the Kowloon ferry dock and the rest
of Hong Kong, barring the Territories.

While Cliff took up his duties with the Army Engineering
Centre in Taiwan, Pema and I became residents of the Prince
Hotel on Kowloon. There we stayed for two months living
on take-away and room service, which Pema soon narrowed
down to ketchup and apple strudel only. She would wake up
each morning and, as soon as she was dressed, climb into the
stroller, point to the door and in her most authoritative tone
say "GO." That was the first English word she uttered, as best
I can remember. Her imagined destination was Victoria Park
and all the climbing frames she could manage with my help
at not-quite-age-two. Under her "Go" instruction, we were
headed for the elevator and all her adoring fans. I would have
to stand on guard to discourage those fingers that found her
sweet, chubby cheeks irresistible to the pinch.

"Bye, bye," she would wave to the audience when we left
the elevator.

"Oh, she even speaks Chinese," came the chorus from the
closing door. I figured "Bye, bye" must have been a universal
expression of departure. I heard all the Hong Kong Chinese
using it as if it were native Cantonese.

~

Come the end of July we had found and moved into our
flat near the Peak on Hong Kong Island within a short drive
to another park full of swings and slides and climbing frames.
In September 1986 we flew home to complete the stateside
adoption and finalize her United States citizenship. This took
place at Chicago's famous Cook County Courthouse, the one
with the even more famous Calder sculpture perched at the

entrance. We had a hard time persuading Pema that it was not meant for climbing. Just across the street at McDonald's was her first introduction to panhandlers. The young gentleman was wearing dreadlocks and sporting a boom box. Pema immediately made friends with him, conversation aside, and after a whole lot of gesturing, he bowed out with a small contribution and a high five.

For the sake of speed and efficiency, Muriel Shennan, our guardian-angel in Springfield, Illinois and Coordinator of Inter-country Adoption, Department of Children and Family Services, recommended the Chicago lawyer Nick Stevenson, senior partner at Mandel, Lipton and Stevenson Limited whom we fondly referred to as "the fixer." Without his experience and influence we would probably still be in the Courthouse. He had made all the arrangements for us to go before the judge for the last adoption formalities. Before we could step inside the judge's chambers, however, Mr. Stevenson made a point of holding out the documents for Pema to touch before we could proceed, since it was Pema who was supposed to be petitioning the county clerk for citizenship. Once he managed to get the papers back from Pema, no small task because she thought they were a gift, he made official note of her tiny hand print and was off to rescue another adoptive family from the tedium of government bureaucracy.

I remember that Judge Wachowski's face was kind. It was obvious to me that he wanted everyone to feel comfortable in his chambers. There was even a little shelf set facing him just in front of his judge's bench, which a clerk helped Pema climb so that she could face him. The judge introduced himself and stated the purpose of our visit. Then he turned to Pema.

"Do you want to live with these people?" he asked, pointing

toward us seated some distance behind her. I had not expected this line of questioning directed at Pema and began to panic. Would she be able to understand his Chicago accent and what he was asking her? And would she be able to answer? She was not yet actually talking. She managed rather successfully to have all her needs met by gesturing. I knew this was one of those developmental issues I would have to address as soon as we were back in Hong Kong. In fact, I had already phoned The Matilda Child Development Center to see if there was an opening and had made an appointment for us.

Before we left Hong Kong for the States we had filed the required formal progress report to SICW, as follows. According to all the books on child development, Pema was developing normally. At age 22 months, she weighed 25 pounds and was 31 inches tall. The birth marks were fast fading, as we were told they would. She was happy and well-adjusted, was outgoing with both children and adults, had good eye and hand coordination, was sure-footed and loved climbing Hong Kong's endless hills. Potty-training was coming along well; she rarely soiled her nappy. She liked to dress herself. She liked to imitate our activities, like talking on the telephone, opening locks or using the typewriter. She showed little interest in TV and actually ran from the room when the Muppets appeared. She loved to listen to music, especially western classical and modern jazz. On the downside, she was showing frustration when she found she couldn't do things as fast or efficiently as Mommy and Daddy, although this was normal for her age. Also she seemed absolutely fearless until she discovered her shadow, but that seemed to have run its course. We had to report that she appeared to understand almost all we said to her, but she herself had only a very basic working vocabulary. Her physical development was taking precedence over her verbal. We were looking into that.

The judge's question, "Do you want to live with these people?" seemed to hang in the air like one of those empty cartoon bubbles. After a time, he adjusted his glasses and turned his attention to the pages of the document in front of him. I was on the edge of my seat, ready to launch myself at the judge when Pema turned around, took a good straight-faced look at us, and nodded "yes." Then she reached out to us to be relieved of her perch.

Clutching the freshly stamped and sealed documents which the judge had passed to us from the warmth of his hand well-shaken, we hurried to what we thought was the final step in the process. At the Federal Building across the street we had to present the adoption papers in order to apply for immigration and her U. S. passport. This is where the fast train engineered by our lawyer came to a screeching halt, as they say.

We were summarily informed by the Immigration official that no way could Pema leave the U. S. until she had held residence for seven years. When Cliff asked to talk to the official he had spoken with by phone from Hong Kong, our man across the desk said that he had no knowledge of such a person. Besides he was firm in his reading of the law.

"For her to acquire citizenship," he said, as if reading from some manual, "the applicant in question must be required to reside in the U. S. for a period of at least seven years." As if on cue, Pema began to squirm in my lap.

"That's not what I was told by your colleague," Cliff said. But the guy was adamant about his knowledge of the law. Cliff argued that the one he spoke to from Hong Kong said he could get us in and out of immigration pronto since we were expatriates and permanent residents overseas, so long as Pema remained with us in our household wherever we lived. Yes, we had to come to the States to process the U.S. adoption and her citizenship which we were doing now during our annual home-leave. Cliff said that he was led to believe that the man he spoke with was a man who could get things done.

"What you are asking is not possible," the officer in front of us argued, "and the contact you are referring to is not here." At this point, Cliff scooted down in his chair and leaned way back extending his 5-foot-6 –inch frame out under the desk to match what appeared to be the guy's 6-foot-6-inch frame. He put his hands in his pockets letting his corduroy jacket fall open. I had seen my husband do this when he knew the game was about up and he was on the verge of winning the argument.

"Never mind," Cliff said. "I'll see him at Foggy Bottom when I fly to D. C. tomorrow." The suggestion that Cliff had connections with the State Department must have set off an alarm, because suddenly another officer sitting at the desk across the aisle was sitting up and taking notice.

"He's upstairs," the man said and handed our man a note. He frowned at the note, pulled the papers on his desk together, stood up abruptly, and mumbled something about going upstairs. In less than half an hour, or the time it took Pema to finish a box of animal crackers and take a little nap sitting in my lap, he was back at his desk.

"This has never been done before. I don't know who you are or who you know to get this done." His look said I don't want to know either. "But it's been taken care of. Come back in a week for the formal swearing-in ceremony."

This wasn't the first time Cliff had been mistaken for a

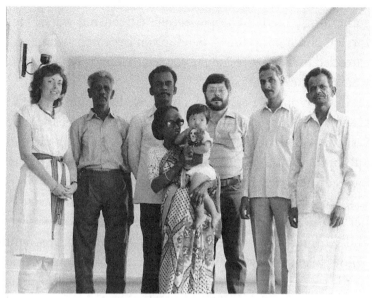

Pema with her "staff," from left
Bonnie, James, Muthiswamy, Cliff, Balraj, Muniappa, and Margret

government operative. In those days, everyone who worked overseas was suspected of being connected with the Agency somehow or the other. Spooks popped up at dinner parties, diplomatic events, and even one poetry reading I remember. They would seek Cliff out because of his first-hand, up-to-date knowledge of local conditions in remote locations. His work involved training, assisting and troubleshooting problems for the customers. As such, it was possible for him to travel to sometimes sensitive areas unnoticed, areas not open to the spooks. And they were interested in his collection of locally sourced maps. More than once he was able to point out errors in theirs. This was before Google Maps and the National Reconnaissance Office.

As a footnote to all that hassle, some two years later

something called "a compassionate citizenship waiver" for foreign children up for U. S. adoption became law and was extended to families resident overseas, so long as both parents were American citizens.

In the required passage of a week, we had returned to the Courthouse with Pema, dressed in her pink, white, and blue OshKosh B'Gosh bib overalls. Everyone else was dressed appropriately in Naturalization Oath attire. When the clerk banged the gavel, Pema stood up straight and tall between Cliff and me with our arms interlaced behind her to steady her on the bench. The clerk spoke earnestly about the rights and responsibilities of U. S. citizenship. All of us, red and yellow, black and white, were instructed to repeat the same words together in one patriot melting pot at that auspicious moment. "I hereby declare, on oath, that I absolutely and entirely renounce and abjure all allegiance and fidelity to any foreign prince, potentate, state or sovereignty….."At about the end of the first paragraph, sounded out more or less in unison in 100 or so different accents, our daughter lost patience and was ready to go. After many rounds of hugs and kisses from Cliff's family in mid-state Illinois, we were headed back to Hong Kong.

JUNGLE GLIDER

Above the cut and thrust
I fly out of the canopy
and lift, a hang glider
stretched between death and hope.

The baby sleeps just here
tucked under my skin
her fists folded against
each new threat.

Homeless again
we climb to merciful heaven
shining through the canopy.
She is so good
wrapped in my flight
I take her for granted.
Under siege,
I forget her lustre.

Chapter 21

BACK HOME IN SINGAPORE
AND THEREAFTER

By the spring 1988 we were packing for the move back to Singapore, back to the welcoming arms of family friends and colleagues, familiar work for Cliff, work awaiting me at the Botanic Gardens and the National Museum, and a ready-made play-group for Pema. I tried to convey Pema's experience of Singapore in this letter to Sr. Dionysia.

71 Holland Road, #01–03
Singapore 1025
5 June 1988

Sr. Dionysia, M.C.
Missionaries of Charity
Shanta Bhavan
Tindharia, Darjeeling
India

My dear Sr. Dionysia,
   Hardly a day goes by that we do not think of you, of the children and the goodness of your work. Cliff will soon be on his way to

Calcutta with the hope that he can visit with you personally. I must believe that he will find you in perfect health and as busy as ever. My only sadness is that Pema and I cannot see you as well. I wish so much for you to be able to share our joy and love in Pema. If only you could see her growing so beautiful and bright and loving. At least Cliff will have photos to give you. We do hope to join him on some future trip to India.

After almost two years in Hong Kong, we've happily settled again in Singapore which I believe is a much kinder place for children. The pace is slower and easier and more tuned to the needs of children. Also there's a solid family orientation in the dominant Chinese culture. Children are still valued as something precious here. Although Pema continues to miss her friends in Hong Kong, she has made the adjustment to her new home quite well. After many months of saying she wanted to go back, now more frequently she asks that her Hong Kong friends come to visit her here.

She is tucked away at playschool this morning, at Mrs. Miller's bungalow in Rochester Park—where the rain trees stretch wide over the garden spread with trikes and painting easels and tables lumped with blue play-dough. This is cooking day, so I expect some chubby-fingered creation like Treacle Tarts or Rock Buns from Mrs. Miller's oven. Mostly Pema and the other little girls focus their doings around the Wendy House. This is the great age of pretend, you know. And sometimes I have to remind her that I am the mommy.

At Christmas, she played the part of "chief angel" in the school Nativity program and led the tots' chorus in "Away in the Manger…the little old Jesus lay down his sweet head…." By the night of the event, she had memorized everybody's lines so that she managed to fill in for an errant Wise Man, too. I blush to say it, but she grows more wonderful by the centimeter. At present she's a bubbling spring of conversation and has reached the stage in which questions come such as, "Mommy, what do feelings look like?"

Sometimes, however, she brings her outdoor voice indoors along with her three-and-a-half-year-old exuberance, and things get a bit wound up, especially in the vicinity of Daddy's office. Her favorite companion is a black and white tomcat who followed us home. Fat Choy tolerates being cuddled, swaddled, stuffed, and hauled around in all manner of conveyances, as well as less gentle demonstrations of affection, and so we decided that he was durable enough to stay.

Sunday seems to be her favorite day, especially when Daddy's home. I take her to Sunday School at St. George's Church (Anglican) and then her daddy takes her to Tumble Tots, a mild form of gymnastics. Her preference has always been for doing *things— bicycling, climbing, swinging, swimming, whatever makes for action. Even so she always enjoys quiet story-time and has a few videos that hold her attention, as well. She can make the letter "P" clear as can be and will soon have control of the rest of her name. She knows her numbers up to seven, and I must say that I have not coaxed or prodded her in any of these skills. She's quite independent-minded and does everything in her own good time.*

We thank God for the miracle of Pema's presence in our life, and to you, Dear Sr. Dionysia, our hearts' thanks as well. Please keep us in your prayers, as we keep you forever in ours.

Love,

Bonnie, Cliff and Pema

> *Madras*
> *15.8.88*

Dear Bonnie, Cliff and Pema,

It's lovely to look at the charming face of Pema in the picture before me. I am happy she's well with you. The happiness you can give to her is visible on her face.

Indeed I was surprised and happy when I saw Cliff standing at the door of Shishu Bhavan – Madras.

Thinking of you, my thoughts fly back to Tindharia and I remember the tender days of Pema. She was an angel always at Our place. The miracles that have worked for each little angel in that place I can never forget whole of my life. The starting of that home and each incident has made a great impact in my own life. Pema is one of the blooming buds in the history. May God fill your hearts with unending joy, peace, and love.

If Cliff ever happens to visit Hazaribagh – I would like you to visit Francis – my brother who is a teacher in St. Francis High School.

I am looking forward to your next visit and more anxious to see Pema with my own eyes.

I am grateful to you for the memory of me you cherish in your hearts and the loving bond which Pema created in uniting us.

With Best wishes and kisses to Pema,
Sr. M. Dionysia

~

So much of revealing the true-to-life past feels like blood-letting. Just open a vein, someone has said, and the past flows out full of regrets, if we stay true to our memories. There were times when I lost my temper, my face a red fire-ball flashing at hers, her chin tucked in facing away from me. That's when I would think that Sr. Margaret Mary may have been right. I wasn't worthy of this sacred charge.

Did I fuss at Pema? Yes. Was I impatient with her? Yes. Did I get angry and yell at her? Yes. Did I spank her? No. Well, once I turned around to her when she was seated in the back of the car and gave her a good smack on the cheek. I thought she was being rude to her Dad who was driving. That is how I remember it.

That is also how I remembered my precious cousin Anna Mae reacting to my rudeness directed at her mother, my Aunt Carlton. I must have been about the same age as Pema, about 6, I think. Anna Mae turned around from the driver's seat with fire in her eyes and let me have a stinging one on the cheek. I remembered how shocked and hurt I was at the time. And in that replay, I made a promise to myself that I would never physically hurt my daughter again. If anything stirs tears in me now it is the very thing that upset my mother and caused her to erect all those protective walls around me. I cry when I think that Pema might be disappointed or hurt in any way, although growing up with a mostly full-time father has helped provide her with a good measure of confidence and self-protection.

Do I need to spell it out—how very thankful I am for our daughter's birth, for her birth mother, and for her decision to give up her baby? I think how empty my life would be had Pema not been such an essential part of it, empty of her beauty, her big heart, her old soul that had so much to teach me about giving and receiving love.

Pema made even Christmas more meaningful for me. Now when I think of the birth of the Christ child, I associate it with her birth and the promise of newborn babies everywhere. A person more religious than I might make the case for this being God's intention in the birth of Jesus—to give added sacred value to each and every child.

If I could do all those early years over, I would carry with me into every hour of every day the awareness of her miraculous presence and how it invested our family life with the true meaning and purpose it needed. I would give thanks for her being the cool headed, no-nonsense person she has turned out to be, for all the doors she opened for me, all the adventures in exotic places we shared, the magic spell she has cast over all my days. And I would advise all parents, not just adoptive ones, to hold their children in sacred trust.

Bonnie, Pema, and Cliff vacationing in Maesa Valley, northern Thailand

~

Did we live happily ever after? If happiness can be defined as loving, enduring relationships that span the globe, then yes. I think Pema's self-description answers the question, too. She likes to say that she is "a people person." I attribute that assessment to the experience of learning to live with so many people of so many ages, races, languages, and ethnic groups in four different orphanages in India, plus four equally diverse countries over the course of her first 10 years of life.

Pema grew up to love horses and world travel. You might remember that her first word in English was "go." While I would have preferred hanging around for room service atop Hong Kong's Prince Hotel, she would climb into her push-chair first thing in the morning and point at the door. She could pack her own suitcase by age five. At about the same age, she won a photo contest with Tumble Tots and took her parents with her to Chiang Mai, Thailand on an elephant ride. At age seven, she learned to ride horse-back at the Polo Club in Singapore. At ten, she fell off a horse while riding at Fraser's Hill in Malaysia and broke her arm. Soon after our return to Singapore, she was back on horse-back at the Polo Club stables.

~

When her Dad quit Asia in 1995 and moved us to the States, we arrived in time for Pema to start 6th grade. We were visiting friends in the Nashville area with an eye to settling there. One Saturday afternoon Cliff and his good friend Doc, the Medic attached to his unit in Vietnam, were telling each other war stories, as was their custom. They were crossing Second Avenue in downtown Nashville when Doc mentioned an incident in a village in Vietnam. Cliff froze in the middle of the street and essentially blacked out standing up. Doc helped him reach the curb and sit down. He explained to the tipsy onlookers that Cliff was having a flashback.

Cliff had been transported back some 30 years to May 1968 when his unit had been on a village sweep patrol in Vietnam. What they found was a hamlet on the edge of rice paddies and a hooch filled with the sounds of villagers in mourning. They were beckoning his team to come in. Cliff had followed his platoon commander inside and saw him take off his helmet and drop his weapon on its sling.

"You don't want to see this," he told Cliff. Cliff stepped past him and saw a table in the middle of the room. The table held two bodies, an old man, probably the village elder, and a young girl, perhaps eight or nine years old. Cliff too lowered his rifle on its sling and removed his helmet. He made the sign of the cross, said Hail Marys, and bowed his head until Doc came in and said there was nothing he could do. The little girl had a severe head wound. A part of the back of her skull was gone. Even though Cliff had no children, the experience affected him just as it did the men standing around him who had children. He would never be able to look at another Vietnamese child again without seeing that innocent little girl.

This tragic memory had been locked away for years, only showing up in the occasional nightmare or flashback but never entering his consciousness until that day in 1995. After a while, Cliff recovered somewhat and Doc pointed out that that embedded memory was why he was so determined to have Pema. He had always known he wanted to adopt an Asian child, a girl. He just never realized why until then.

~

Back in the States, our family travel to exotic places came to an end, but Pema carried on. Cliff and I may not have been with her, but I am convinced she always traveled in the company of a fleet of angels. There was a trip with classmates to Europe in middle school, back home with us to Singapore in high school, a semester-abroad in Ghana as part of her undergraduate studies at Indiana University, an extended visit after college with Aunt Jane in Dharamsala (where Jane has been attached to the Dalai Lama's community since 1986). There Pema joined Students for a Free Tibet and during the Beijing Olympics marched with Tibetan monks toward Tibet by way of Amritsar and Delhi, a 600-mile protest march to raise awareness of the plight of Tibetans under Chinese rule. Pema was the one providing the English pod-casting. The Indian military stopped them before they could reach the border. She was able to do all that hassle-free because of her "person of Indian origin" passport that entitled her to all the rights of Indian citizenship with the exception of voting rights and ownership of farm land.

An internship for her Masters in International Human Rights at the University of Denver took Pema back to India, Calcutta, and Delhi, to work with an NGO fighting trafficking of women and children. This time she took out a weekend to visit Darjeeling and her first home at Mother Teresa's Shanta Bhavan. One of the workers there told her that she actually remembered Pema from the time she was there as a baby. And she also remembered the American couple who came to adopt her.

Since that visit, much has come to light that may help complete the story. Aunt Jane has reported that a friend found records of two Tibetan girls enrolled in the government school who gave birth to baby girls at Victoria Hospital in November 1984. Do I want to return to Darjeeling to pursue their whereabouts or shall I wait for Pema to do that? She is so invested in the here and now that she seems quite comfortable to leave her distant past in Darjeeling.

Only very much later when trying to verify all the historical facts in the book did I learn that Mother, too, was deep in her own agony over the distance she felt from God at the very moment when I was seeking Him "long distance."

For longer than anyone knows, Mother rose every morning at 4:40 a.m. to lay her life in loving service to the poorest of the poor before her Christ, whom she perceived to be unresponsive too much of the time. She chose to share this information with very few. It came to light only when her letters and private papers were published in 2007 in *Mother*

Teresa, Come Be My Light, The Private Writings of the "Saint of Calcutta," edited and with commentary by Father Brian Kolodiejchuk, M.C. postulator of her cause for sainthood and director of the Mother Teresa of Calcutta Center in San Ysidro, California. It was never her intention for these letters to find print. She had begged all her correspondents to destroy whatever they had received from her.

It broke my heart to hear her confess that she had to wear a happy face to hide the sadness in her soul. This had been going on for years, in spite of the enormous success of her Missionaries of Charity, the world's most celebrated charitable organization in the name of Jesus Christ. She spoke of her interior struggle, on the one hand knowing that it brought the Sisters and others encouragement to hear her speak of God's work, but on the other feeling emptiness, total separation from God and yet a painful longing for Him. More than one of the priests she confided in made the association with St. John of the Cross, the great mystic who believed himself incapable of knowing God's light and love because of his immersion in the purifying "crucible" of these mystical sufferings, his "dark night of the soul." Although she eschewed any comparison between his and her own dark plight, I found her words to be an honest confession of the human condition, and I took great strength from them.

During that same period when we were desperately trying to get our Pema, Mother's congregation was deeply worried about her declining health. During her visit with Pope John Paul II in May 1983, she suffered cardiac arrest and had to remain in Rome for a month on forced vacation in order to recover. After that, they noticed that she had lost her lively step. The vertebral problem she refused to treat medically

Pema with her mom and dad in the Hong Kong flat, Christmas 1986

caused her stoop to be more pronounced. She seemed a pale shadow of her radiant self. Chronic headaches had been her constant companion for many years and now, angina pectoris.

She did not slow her pace. On Christmas Day 1984, despite having a fever, she went to Ethiopia to do what she and her Sisters could for the terrible famine. In January, she launched a hectic one-month tour of China, Hong Kong, and Macao. Her itinerary in 1983 and 1984 included Bangladesh, Tanzania, Kenya, Italy, Germany, England, the U.S., Latin America, Poland, Australia, and Hong Kong. In 1984 alone, she visited 50 of her 118 foundations in India.

At age 75, after 35 years on the job and the establishment of 233 foundations staffed by 2,500 Sisters and Fathers spread over six continents, she was longing to step down. She fervently urged the Holy See to replace her in her role as superior general in the upcoming election. She pleaded the case in her letters.

"The conviction of my nothingness," she wrote, "has made the work & the whole Society completely his. He will do still greater things if He finds somebody more nothing than I ... I will be happy, very happy to be free—and to be just a simple Sister in the Community—after nearly 35 years." Once again in 1985, she was overwhelmingly re-elected. And she remained head of her congregation until six months before her death in 1997.

~

With a very few well-publicized exceptions, all the world would agree that if there ever were a saint, Mother Teresa would be such a one. During her nearly 50 years' service to the poorest of the poor, she became an icon of compassion and a beacon world-wide to the homeless, the diseased and dying, the multitudes nobody else was willing to care for. Only one year following her death, Pope John Paul II must have recognized her unique worthiness when the Vatican waived the five-year waiting period after death normally required to consider a candidate for sainthood.

In 2002, the church recognized the first miracle that led to her beatification the following year. Reaching the status required for canonization or sainthood, however, had been delayed for lack of proof of a bona fide miracle number two. Thousands of personal reports of supernatural favors attributed to Mother's intercession worldwide had documented the search, according to Father Brian. Not until 2015 did the Vatican announce recognition of a second miracle. On September 4, 2016, Pope Francis wasted no more time in formally canonizing her "Saint Teresa of Kolkata" in the open-air mass that brought hundreds of thousands from all over the world to celebrate the life of Mother Teresa in St. Peter's Square.

Among the infinite number of miracles proposed over those 17 years, we would be pleased to offer yet another miracle, the prayerful intervention of Mother Teresa in our adoption process on the night of September 3, 1985. Given all the circumstances, all the mysterious forces working around the world on our behalf, including the disembodied hand and the voice saying "wait," for which I have no natural explanation, we have always believed our Pema came to us by way of a miracle.

COVENANT

And when that one bright star
took its place in the sky
to illuminate Love,
who would have guessed
all that was to follow?

Who would have thought
moving pictures and Mozart,
Mendel's garden, Cezanne's mountains,
Olympic speed and moon walks,
domesticated cats, chocolate kisses,
microscope, telescope, books!

That it would come to this,
such delight in discovering –
say, the dulcimer her Daddy made
when he was a boy
and the land she was born in,
one of countless unknowns.

Who would have thought
there could be so much
between Earth and Heaven to love
or so much grace
for the renewing of it
year after miraculous year.

(in loving memory of Mother Teresa)

Chapter 22

EPILOGUE

P*ema writes about her one and only return trip to Darjeeling in winter 2010, as follows:*

~

Meghan and I met up at Bagdogra, the nearest airport to Darjeeling 90 km away, from internships in Delhi and Calcutta, respectively. We each wanted a weekend getaway to escape the hustle and bustle of the cities. Meghan, fellow grad student, suggested the idea over G chat on-line. I agreed immediately. I had yet to find my niche in Calcutta, and I longed for familiarity and a friend. It was almost an after-thought that I would be returning for the first time to my birthplace—to a place so steeped in memory for my parents. For me, it was more of a holiday weekend jaunt to the moun-tains than a profound journey of self-discovery or coming to terms with being adopted.

It was the end of February 2010 and Darjeeling was shrouded in dense fog. Meghan and I made our way to our hotel and were met by the manager bearing a mountain of blankets and a hot water bottle for each of us. We dined on *chow mein* and *momos*, Tibetan-styled dumplings, and fell fast asleep after a long day of travel by taxi, plane, four by four, and foot.

Our first full day in Darjeeling, we had breakfast on the veranda. On a clear day, we would have had a perfect view of Kanchenjunga. For this trip, a postcard's rendering would have to suffice. We walked to the zoo and the mountaineering museum, visited the stores in the Chowrasta, and walked up and down the narrow streets contemplating purchasing knock-off North Face and Mountain Hardwear gear. We tasted teas at Nathmulls and found ourselves at the Windamere in time for afternoon tea and biscuits. I imagined my parents, Aunt Jane, and their gang of friends traipsing about the same places 26 years earlier. It was surreal in an oddly comforting way.

We were mid-way into our second day, and it was time. Armed with the *Lonely Planet* guidebook, we set out for the Missionaries of Charity. We passed it twice before noticing the sign out front. We rolled back the corrugated metal gate and walked into the courtyard. It was nearly empty except for several Sisters who were chatting. Meghan and I walked up to them and I blurted out, "I was a baby here." The Sisters gave reassuring smiles and ushered us into a small room.

We sat down and I recounted my story as best I could. I had heard it many times told by both parents and by my Aunt Jane. I can't recall the version I told that day. To be honest, I can't recall much of that hour, or was it 30 minutes or two hours? I do know that I felt at ease and comforted. The Sisters served us chai tea and showed us pictures of other children, like me, who had returned. There were children from Belgium and Switzerland and other European countries and several from Canada. The Sisters asked if I had come looking for my biological family. I said no. They speculated that I could easily learn more by going down to Tindharia to the orphanage there. I smiled and thanked them. I asked about Sister Dionysia and was told that she was in service in rural Andhra Pradesh, one of India's poorest states.

Nightfall was fast approaching and Meghan and I needed to leave. The Sisters handed us each a Miraculous Medal, a Mother Teresa of Kolkata Medal, and a prayer card. They told us to come back the next time we were in Darjeeling. They walked us to the rolling, corrugated metal gate and blessed us both. And with that, the return to my first home was over.

ABOUT THE AUTHOR

Bonnie Tinsley is the author of numerous books, including *The World in a Garden: Singapore's Gardens by the Bay* (Marshall Cavendish, 2016), a beautifully illustrated picture book celebrating Singapore's award-winning botanical and architectural wonder located near the South China Sea. This is the fourth book she has authored on Singapore's national gardens.

After 15 years' residence in Southeast Asia, Bonnie and her family returned to the states to make their home in Tennessee in 1996. She is presently Adjunct Professor of Latin at Middle Tennessee State University, Department of Foreign Languages and Literature in Murfreesboro. For more information visit her online at bonnietinsley.com.